MARCELO BIELSA'S LEEDS UNITED

Love. Heidi Hough

LUFC - Marching on Together!

MARCELO BIELSA'S LEEDS UNITED

HEIDI HAIGH

HEIDI'S DEDICATION

This book is dedicated to my Leeds United family as Leeds fans look after their own. The support of those fans who have helped me through the challenging start my family and I have had to 2019 is immeasurable and I am eternally grateful. MOT!

Heidi Haigh – A fanatical Leeds United supporter of over 50 years.

AUTHOR OF THE FOLLOWING BOOKS:

Follow Me and Leeds United

Once a Leeds fan, Always a Leeds fan

The Sleeping Giant Awakens, Leeds United 2016-17

Back to Reality, Leeds United 2017-18

Co-author with Andrew Dalton of *The Good, The Bad and The Ugly of Leeds United*, *Leeds United in the 1980s*

Website: www.followmeandleedsunited.co.uk

Twitter: @FollowMeAndLUFC

Facebook: Follow Me and Leeds United

Instagram: lufcheidi

First Published in Great Britain in 2019 by DB Publishing,
an imprint of JMD Media Ltd

ISBN 9781780916019

Printed and bound in the UK

TABLE OF CONTENTS

FOREWORD

LOYAL LEEDS UNITED FANS – STEVE AND BEVERLEY SMITH, BOURNEMOUTH WHITES

We are looking forward to next season already. I started supporting Leeds as a young lad of five. I can remember them playing in all white and winning Division Two in 1963/64 and thinking how pristine they looked in that white kit and that was it I was hooked, that's the team for me. The first games I went to were in the season 1974/75; I was 15 at the time, still in school and can remember my first home game against Ipswich. We won 2-1 and I stood on the Gelderd Road end. I was walking home from school on the Friday and two mates pulled up beside me and asked me if I wanted to go to Leeds v Ipswich. They picked me up at 5am as I jumped out of my bedroom window because I didn't tell my parents about it. Off we set in an 850cc mini; the two lads were called Kev Charlton and Nick Maidment. I will never forget that game as it took us seven hours to get there and we had a few pints of milk off peoples' doorsteps along the way. We got back home after midnight where I climbed back through the window and still, to this day, my parents never knew I had gone to the football. In those days I went to as many as I could, mostly the London games and the Midlands. I met Bev in 1989 and converted her there and then to Leeds, to the dismay of her dad, who had a fond spot for Wimbledon and Portsmouth. The rest, as they say, is history Heidi as we continued to go to as many games as we could, despite starting up my own business, having a mortgage etc.

We became home season ticket holders and then away ticket holders simply because it was easier to get tickets for matches as we just didn't have the time to get on the club website for them. This was the best thing we have ever done. We've got used to the getting up at 4am for home matches now after all this time, travelling in excess of 20,000 miles a season home and away and still get the buzz of a match day. We have met so many lovely people along the way who have become great friends.

This season has been by far the best we have played in a decade. A rollercoaster ride from start to finish it had it all, highs, lows and everything thrown in between. Leeds have played some pulsating football at times, battering teams into submission, and then other games we failed to turn up when it mattered. But that is what you get with supporting Leeds you never know what is going to happen. The only thing certain is the amazing support that turns up week in week out across the country that will never be beaten by anybody. You asked us what Leeds means to Bev and me? That's a simple question to answer – everything Leeds United AFC is our way of life and will continue to the day we die and beyond. There is no other football club in the world that even comes close to having what we have in the LUFC family. Loyalty, injustices against us, hated by everyone and the sheer bloody mindset that we will get back to the promised land. See you soon my lovely, love Steve & Bev – on and on MOT.

MARCELO BIELSA'S LEEDS UNITED

PROLOGUE BY HEIDI HAIGH

When Leeds United started looking for a new manager, the name being mentioned was Marcelo Bielsa. Having not heard of him, I immediately did some research then took a step back to look at the whole picture. What I did see stirred my inner emotions, because he reminded me of Don Revie, who was manager of the greatest Leeds United side I have been privileged to see. Having followed Leeds United for over 50 years, I have seen the successes of that team in person and they are responsible for me being the die-hard Leeds fan I am today. When I heard that Marcelo Bielsa watches all the videos of other teams, analysing everything, I remembered Don Revie and his many dossiers. Preparation is the key and at least both of them have taken time to know about the opposition. Both were totally immersed in what they believed in, which was good to see. The more I read about Marcelo Bielsa, the more I wanted him to come to Leeds and was more than happy when he did.

I met Marcelo Bielsa briefly at our pre-season game at York when I managed to get a quick photo with him as he went into the ground. I even made the official Leeds United recording at that time; maybe it is the beret that gave it away? The season became one of the best we have had for many a year and some of the football we saw was sublime. All I want to see are the players having pride in playing for the shirt which shows they want the same success that the fans do and are happy to connect with the fans. A successful Leeds United will be a great reward for the Leeds fans who have stuck with them through thick and thin. Marcelo Bielsa, as our manager, brought us so close to that success, which faltered at the last moment when we ended up third in the league and lost out in the play-offs. Players who had been written off by some fans performed out of their skins under his guidance, and their interaction with the fans became second nature. The team worked tirelessly in the community too, which has long been needed.

Celebrations on the terraces with many last-minute goals contributing to these have been captured in photos that are included in this book. The Leeds fans, as ever, have been loyal and supported Leeds in their thousands wherever we went. Any beam backs at Elland Road were also sold out as well as the away tickets, which was amazing considering the amount of times Leeds were live on TV. Being on TV doesn't matter to us Leeds fans because we would rather be at a game supporting our team.

Bielsa's first season as manager of Leeds United has been written about in this book by me as a fan for the fans. This takes in my travels to friendlies, home and away games and is based on my blog *Follow Me and Leeds United*. The blog is shared with many Leeds fans around the world, some who can't get to games but who look forward to reading my honest account. I look forward to meeting up with many of these fans again next season. Enjoy the read.

FANS COMMENTS

Peter Hillick   A great read as always and good luck with the book Derby 11.8.18.

Alo Keating   Great photos Heidi and great blog as usual - MOT Derby 11.8.18.

Richard Ainley   Great blog as ever Heidi Haigh Derby 11.8.18.

David Robinson   Hi mate – greetings from Singapore – just wanted to say love your website and Leeds blog – MOT.

Kevin Pawley   Nice to have you back, missed your blog for the 1st two games ... MOT Bolton 14.8.18.

Diane Wagstaff Cook   Lovely, from a Leeds fan living in Fairford, Gloucestershire Rotherham 18.8.18.

Pete Lupton, Australia   Just want to say how much I look forward to your blogs. It takes me back to when I travelled home and away on the coaches. Especially love the photos of the fans at the Peacock before the game because that for me was a massive part of the #lufc experience. Have a great night at Swansea Rotherham 18.8.18.

Dick Wesselman   Love to read and see the photos as a Dutch Leeds fan Swansea 21.8.18.

Christian Ellsmore   Great report as always. Love reading about your day out Swansea 21.8.18.

Lynsey Elizabeth   Love your posts. I can't get to some away games as you know and a lot last couple of seasons due to personal circumstances. I certainly look forward to your posts especially away matches. Keep doing what you do. You do amazing, there's a lot of fans all over the world love your posts xx Norwich 25.8.18.

Dave Luke   I can't believe there's people out there giving you abuse Heidi. Unfortunately I am one of the many supporters who don't get to all the away games these days and I look forward to your blogs and looking through your photographs. These people who give you abuse are not genuine supporters and are people the club could do without. Keep up the good work you do for the thousands of people that look forward to reading your blogs. You are a credit to Leeds United, Marching on Together Norwich 25.8.18.

Sinéad Denton   As an overseas fan I am grateful for the time and effort you put in to making these posts and sharing your photos - always nice to spot familiar faces! I'd ignore any negativity because there are so many more of us who are grateful and look forward to your posts; who cares if it pops up two or three times in different groups, we can all scroll by! Norwich 25.8.18.

Brian Gunn These blogs are always brilliant. Thanks   #mot Norwich 25.8.18.

Angela Donaghue Hiya love you do an amazing job love all your photos and blogs. I can't get home as you know my problems plus live so far away now in Liverpool so I always look forward to your blogs and photos, makes me feel back at home where I belong. Miss home so much so very sad thanks MOT.

Kevin Raymond Jones I love to read and see the photos, thank you for your hard work.

Steve Townson Love your blogs and photos Heidi as I don't get to games anymore. I can spot old friends in them and your honest write ups give me a true account of how we have played, keep them coming.

Andrew Plenderleith You should be awarded a damehood double H. Keep up the fantastic work you do x.

Ilsf Andy You carry on doing what you do best Heidi and that's doing what you're doing, long may you continue.

Laura Moore, *Warwickshire Whites Supporters Group.*

Fully support you and your blog!! Will continue approving your posts in the Whites group. You're a gem Heidi. Marching on TOGETHER xx Swansea 25.8.18.

Karl Domonkos You provide a fantastic pictorial story of every game Heidi and you're a top person too. Keep up the good work and I look forward to seeing your next blog. One of Leeds finest you are so don't forget that #mot.

Billy Gallagher I enjoy reading your blog and viewing your pics but love meeting up more when I can. It was nice to see you at Swansea on Tuesday xx MOT.

Sue Holmes I read all your blogs and feel as though I am at the game, keep writing Heidi you do an amazing job.

Richard Hartley As I live a long way away from ER these reports and photos are great for me and allow me to remember some of the experiences from my youth. You do a great job Heidi and will always have my support.

Thomas Barrett Fair play to ya Heidi, love your blog, when you can't get to games it's great reading them and great photos, MOT!!!!

Nick Chatham Keep up the great work Heidi, it gives us Leeds fans that live in Australia a great insight to what's happening. I have been in Australia for nearly 12 years now and hanker for the past, when I was a season ticket holder in the good, bad and indifferent times. Once Leeds, always Leeds.

Ken Marston

As an American fan, I really appreciate all the pics from both the home and road matches. I'll make it across the pond eventually, but it's great to see all the different faces and places.

Darren Sutcliffe

Heidi Haigh we all love you & all you do for Leeds Utd Football Club! You are a true loyal supporter in more ways than 1! Not only are you always at the games but you always have a positive view & a big smile for everyone! Just ignore them sad people! Enjoy this year as it's going to be a cracker.

Paul Brace

Heidi you do a great job and I am sure I speak for the majority. Unfortunately you can't keep everyone happy in this world but at the same time it is easy to scroll on by. Keep posting & happy posting MOT.

Michael White

Your pictures capture the atmosphere of the crowd and great supporters; to be honest they gave me a happy feeling to see them. There will be people not able to get to matches who will get so much happiness out of your great efforts, so thank you.

Ted O'Connor

As a big Leeds fan who lives in Ireland I love your blogs. Obviously it's difficult to get to games from here, especially away matches with tickets being scarce. But reading your blogs takes me along on the journey and from the very first line about rising early to the closing lines gives a sense **of** being there and participating.

Steve Barnes

Thanks for your efforts Heidi. Unfortunately these people think that social media allows them to behave like the low life they are. People like me who can no longer go on a regular basis welcome what you do. We are Leeds.

Stephen Mc Phillips

Reading your post-game blogs has become part of my Leeds match ritual. Always enjoy them, keep up the good work. M.O.T Preston 28.8.18.

David Shapiro

Please carry on what you are doing in the way you are doing it and take no notice of the loud but small minority. We love what you do MOT forever xx Preston 28.8.18.

John O'Leary

Cheers Heidi, I live in Cambodia and look forward to your match reviews.

Malcolm Pogue

I read every week in Thailand Heidi lol.

John Doona

Your blogs have replaced reading the newspapers in my Sunday ritual. Keep up the bloody good work Millwall A 15.9.18.

Adrian Ochai

Had to read the whole blog for this particular match. Well worth the ten minute read! Was nice to see you there. You looked great in ye Leeds gear. I was the black fella with the Warwickshire crew near the stairwell. I had the red/black sorta checkered shirt!! Best away day and awesome atmosphere at the Den. Happy with the result which in all fairness I would have taken at the start of play. Back to your matchday blogs.......ye always give a good account with regards to following the team up and down the country. You're another example of being the proper football fan. You pretty much sum up what Leeds fans are all about.....loyal, proud. That's just my wee tribute to ye. Hope to meet ye at a home game at some point this season. Enjoy the rest of our season.....regards, Adrian. Millwall A 15.9.18.

Penny Smallwood — Brilliant reading Heidi it was a great performance also great photos to look at MOT Preston H 18.9.18.

Monica Nuñeza Farag — Wow! As always, beautifully written, Heidi! Thoroughly enjoyed reading this article! Brentford H 6.10.18.

Glenn Aston — Great report carry on the good work!! MOT XX Brentford H 6.10.18.

Bobby Joyce — Heidi - it looks like I just missed you with your nice jumper outside the ground as I entered (without team colours) in the Upper Stand behind the goal where all five goals went in! There were quite a few Leeds fans escorted out near me as they could not control their emotions - I sat on my hands. I listened to you on digital radio Wednesday and laughed how you kept bringing up the 70s and saying you only cared what Leeds do not the opposition - MOT - Merry Xmas and may 2019 be like 1990. Aston Villa A 23.12.18.

Andrew Cleghorn — Merry Christmas and thanks for the posts keep em coming MOT Aston Villa A 23.12.18.

Jeff Way — Thanks Heidi it's great to see us on top I am sure we wouldn't have won this game last season from being two down, still very happy that this season we don't give up till the very end. Merry Christmas to you and your family look forward to hear from you soon MOT Aston Villa A 23.12.18.

Alan Pickersgill — Merry Christmas and thanks for the posts keep em coming.. love reading your reports all the way in Australia MOT Aston Villa A 23.12.18.

Iain Macleod — Excellent report as always Heidi, great hearing about the build-up etc, for us that can't get to away games. And it was definitely a hand ball and penalty, even all the Sky folk agreed. Can't get down to this week's games as travel restrictions from Highland Scotland unfortunately, so probably Derby will be my next one. All the best to you and the family. Cheers. Aston Villa A 23.12.18.

Debbie Fishman

Cheers Heidi Haigh & you got my boy's first win at Villa Park thank you so much. Merry Christmas to you & your lovely family see you Boxing Day & thanks for all your efforts every game, love it & muchly appreciated the time & effort you give for us all xxx Villa A 23.12.18.

Michael Heanue

Great night on and off the pitch. Thank you for the great description of your night and the match Heidi. Derby H 11.1.19.

Iain Macleod

Wow, what a night Heidi, well worth leaving the house at 6.30am and travelling on four trains to be there! Just caught the 7.08am train back north, the voice is slowly coming back! Definitely not offside for early pen and they should have had two red cards! Forshaw was my man of the match, they all played great. Cheers. Derby H 11.1.19.

Michael Burke

Fantastic display by the whole squad… MOT Heidi Haigh Great article, great pics as always. Derby H 11.1.19.

David Flynn

Good Morning Heidi , still keeping up the great work I see!!! Well done MOT Derby H 11.1.19.

Les Wake

Thanks Heidi for yet another great blog. Speaking of great, I thought we totally outclassed the opposition in every department. It was almost cruel. 2-0 didn't do us justice. Agree about Lampard. He needs to put his dummy back in. I was pleased for a friend of mine from here in Adelaide. He was at the game with his son and daughter. It was their first time and a lifelong dream. He messaged me during the game saying the roof was coming off and the atmosphere was fantastic. Derby H 11.1.19.

Christine Armstrong

Thank you for your match report and photos. It keeps me in touch with my beloved club. Was born in Leeds and started following this great club in the sixties but now live in Australia, love to read all the news I can. Keep up the good work, much appreciated. Birmingham A 6.4.19.

Ilsf Andy

Great report Heidi I enjoyed reading that. Aston Villa H 28.4.19.

Paul Jenney

Out of the darkness a light shines. Heidi thank you for your courage. Thank you for carrying on. Thank you for your report and pictures. Always feels like I'm actually at the match. Due to anxiety I can't travel but I travel with you every week. Again a massive thank you. Derby A 11.5.19.

Ann Watson

Thanks Heidi, that even when you're going through difficult times personally, you still take time to write your blog. Keeping you & your family in our thoughts & prayers. Derby A 11.5.19.

CHAPTER 1

FOREST GREEN ROVERS (A) – 17 JULY 2018

Welcome back to the start of the new season and especially to those fans who love reading my blogs and having their photos taken. Last season's blog has just been turned into a new book which has been sent to the publisher and will be out very soon. It is titled *Back to Reality, Leeds United 2017-18* and includes over 150 photos/collages of the fans I've met on our travels and the team. I will have a quota of books to sell myself priced at £12.99. If you want to meet me at a game to buy an autographed copy then please let me know and I will arrange to meet you. The book will also be available on Amazon and hopefully the club shop once again.

As soon as the pre-season programme was announced, I could see it was going to be a very expensive time, with six games in quick succession. As they were all based in this country it also meant a lot of travelling. Forest Green Rovers was the first game that beckoned as this was also a new ground to go to for me. LUSC Fullerton Park and LUSC South Kirkby (both Leeds United Supporters' Club branches) joined together to travel to the game so it was a trip straight there and back. After a good journey down, I waited outside the turnstiles whilst others went into the beer tent outside the away end. After chatting to a few fans who I knew I decided to walk around the ground. As I got to the far end I realised the team had just arrived so headed to the players' entrance. It was noticeable that some of the youngsters looked apprehensive on seeing a group of Leeds fans waiting for them to get off the coach, but they'll soon get used to it.

It was good to be back amongst our fans with lots of familiar faces having their photos taken. As I headed to the turnstiles, I changed my mind as to which one I was going through as I knew I couldn't be searched by a male steward. Another girl came across to my queue and I couldn't believe what I was hearing as the male steward had told her that she couldn't take her contraceptive pill in! Well I've heard it all now, unbelievable. After a search of my bags I was asked if I had any keys so I replied, 'yes my car and house keys.' I wondered why they were included in the search and then remembered I'd seen an email recently saying a new weapon was appearing on the streets which was a key with a blade inside it.

I put my flag up behind the goal and stood with my friends, the Bournemouth and Southampton Whites, who are great company, in readiness for kick-off. With our new manager Marcelo Bielsa recently installed, the team have been training hard under his management and were due to play the full 90 minutes. Personally, I thought that was good to hear, as our fitness levels and bad long-term injuries were a cause of concern for me last season.

The team: Bailey Peacock-Farrell, Luke Ayling, Liam Cooper, Adam Forshaw, Pablo Hernandez, Samuel Saiz, Ezgjan Allioski, Kemar Roofe, Stuart Dallas, Gaetano Berardi, and Kalvin Phillips. Attendance was 3,250, with 1,161 Leeds fans. Leeds won the game 2-1 with goals from Roofe

(16) and Ayling (25). We had signed Lewis Baker, a midfielder, on a season-long loan from Chelsea and Jamal Blackman, a 6ft 7in goalkeeper, also on a season-long loan from Chelsea.

As the team was made up of the same players we had at the end of last season, at least it meant I knew who was who. In the pre-season games it is normally very hard for me to work the players out, especially as I never get a programme anymore, so I need names and numbers on shirts to remind me. We raced into a two-goal lead very early on when Roofe scored our first goal of the season in the 16th minute, followed shortly by Ayling scoring his first goal for us, I believe. Right on half-time Forest Green Rovers pulled one back as Peacock-Farrell was beaten by a shot in the top right-hand corner, right in front of us.

As I was speaking to some of our fans, the conversation turned to my blogs. I said I hadn't been sure if I should put last year's blog into a book before deciding to go ahead with it. Mark said that what I was doing was important; my blog is one of a few that is written about the fans' experience and showing what they go through to support their team. That was so nice to hear and I really appreciate the support as it makes me feel that doing this is worthwhile, as well as sharing my experiences of watching games over a 50+ year span.

As this game was the start of getting ready for the actual season to begin, I wasn't expecting too much. I did like the yellow shirts and blue shorts as there was something about them being in pristine condition that stood out for me. It was also good to be back amongst our fans and catch up with lots of them. Due to a 7pm kick-off and despite a detour to South Kirkby, we made good time getting back to Leeds, although I slept most of the way back.

YORK CITY (A) – 19 JULY 2018

I was struggling to get any enthusiasm for my football due to a workload that had overwhelmed me and made me feel I couldn't do it anymore. I am grateful that I have a chance to recharge my batteries over the summer holiday period. I had driven to the game and managed to get a good parking spot on a nearby street, and as I was there early I headed to the players' entrance. Stix, who co-ordinates the team and events, waved to me from an upstairs window just before the team coach arrived. I thought there was no chance that the coach would be able to get into the area behind the stand but the driver reversed into it with no problems. I decided to film the players getting off the coach and, as expected, there were a lot of the youngsters for this game as it was only two days after the Forest Green game. Bielsa had his photo taken with a young Leeds fan and then two friends of his arrived. He didn't hear me shout him but the girl tapped him on the shoulder and he came back for a photo with me.

I spoke to a few fans and took some photos, then I found out my mum and sister were at Clifton Bingo so headed there to see them before coming back to the ground. I didn't even realise I was in the seats so decided to sit on the front row as I was having severe issues with my feet with pain that came on suddenly at the weekend. It meant I couldn't weight bear for a while and as it

still hadn't settled down it was the best thing to do. As the game kicked off Leeds fans behind the goal started singing they couldn't get in the stand as it was overcrowded at the top as they came up the stairs.

The team: Kamil Miazek, Tom Pearce, Laurens De Bock, Jamie Shackleton, Yosuke Ideguchi, Ronaldo Vieira, Lewis Baker (making his first appearance after signing on loan from Chelsea), Mateusz Klich, Jack Clarke, Jordan Stevens and Ryan Edmondson. Score was 1-1, with Sam Dalby scoring for Leeds (58). Attendance was 4,400, with approximately 2,000 Leeds fans.

I knew Vieira was playing but had no idea until after the game that Klich had played as I didn't bother putting my glasses on. I need to start looking on my phone for the starting line-up I think, as that may help too. York took the lead on 24 minutes after they had come out strongly, and initially we struggled to get any momentum going. It felt like the first half was more of Bielsa seeing some of the youngsters playing who are part of the development squad. Eventually we started getting into the game more and I hoped the fitness levels would help us to improve. We went into the break 1-0 down, although Shackleton was unlucky not to score an equaliser just before the whistle blew.

I'd hung my flag up at the side of the stand but just before half-time the lad behind me said it had fallen down. I went to get it then as I realised fans had decided to untie it so they could see when queuing up for food. I'd not given that a thought so I moved it to the front of the stand instead.

The second half started with three changes made, Will Huffer replaced Miazek, Sam Dalby came in for Stevens and Hugo Diaz for Edmondson. The substitutions made a difference to our performance as the second half belonged to Leeds. Shackleton made some great runs down the side in front of us, beating his man to the byline numerous times. Clarke also showed great potential with an impressive performance. After York hitting the crossbar, it was our turn to do the same with Klich's shot before Dalby put the rebound in to equalise for Leeds. It may have been a 1-1 draw but there were positives to take with some of the individual performances.

This is probably our last visit to Bootham Crescent as York should be moving to a Community Stadium slightly out of town. We always have a good turnout of fans at this fixture and it is always a ground I relished visiting as I used to live near Selby. After we had played in the European Cup Final in Paris, my friend Sue and I went to see York play man u there wearing all our Leeds colours. Some of their fans came from Barnsley, as did some of the Leeds fans, so we stood with the lads we knew.

I was so tired on the way home that I had to pull over three times but better to do it that way and get home safely. Sunday is a very early start with our visit to Southend for our third game in a week so see you there.

SOUTHEND UNITED (A) – 22 JULY 2018

I didn't realise that we were travelling by minibus to this one, with Roy driving us there. We left Leeds at 7am as it was a 2pm kick-off, and after a short stop at Cambridge services we arrived to a very warm Southend. Initially we were going to walk to the sea front but we decided we didn't have enough time to get there and back. As my feet were still giving me trouble it wouldn't have been a good idea. We were directed to the pub near the ground that was for away fans only and it was good to see it had a Leeds scarf hung up behind the bar and Leeds-coloured bunting. It turned out the landlady Michelle was a Leeds fan and so were her parents. Thanks for buying my book *Follow Me and Leeds United* and I look forward to feedback in due course. Michelle later shared some great photos that her parents had of meeting some Leeds players. It was good to see Rudi and his son, who had come from Norway for the game. It is always good to catch up with the Bergen Whites at our pre-season games.

After talking for ages with fans we headed back to the ground where I hung my flag at the back of the stand. As there was a danger of 'flying balls' I decided I would be safer sat behind the goal so joined Andrew and some others. It was roasting and my knees were on fire but it was nice to have some good weather.

The team: Peacock-Farrell, Ayling, Cooper, De Bock (Tyler Roberts (62) making his debut after his transfer in January but had been injured since arriving), Berardi, Forshaw, Phillips, Alioski, Saiz, Dallas and Roofe. Score was 1-1, with Ayling scoring (34). Attendance was 3,815, with 988 Leeds fans.

Leeds played with yellow shirts and blue shorts looking so pristine again. This was another game when Leeds went 1-0 down after 20 minutes and Southend came close to scoring a second. Once again Ayling came to the rescue, scoring his second goal in two games to equalise just before half-time. It was good to see Roberts making his debut eventually too. We came close a couple of times in the final stages of the second half with their goalkeeper making a double save and another kicking one off the line, but the game ended in a draw.

It was nice to have one of their stewards come and ask the Leeds fans if they wanted their water bottles filling up as well as their own stewards. I had been grateful to have a bottle of coke brought for me unexpectedly at half-time by one of the lads sat near me. As he'd brought the others in the group a drink he brought me one too, so thank you.

We had a good run back to Leeds without stopping after a delayed get away due to three of our group not being able to find the minibus. Our next game is Oxford away on Tuesday so see you there.

OXFORD (A) – 24 JULY 2018

I was looking forward to visiting Oxford's new ground today, having visited the Manor Ground in the past. I had treated my daughter Dani to the game today as she's had a tough time recently so it was time to chill out and enjoy getting back to the football. After doing a detour to pick her up we arrived at Elland Road in good time for the coach. Fullerton Park Supporters' Club were sharing a coach with the South Kirkby branch again. We parked up then after a quick visit to Howard's bar for the shop, we returned to the car. On our way back past Billy's statue we saw that the old signs from the shop had been taken down along with the old railings, as they were being replaced with the refurbishment of the club shop. I would have loved to have taken them home but, one, my car isn't big enough and, two, Dani said there was nowhere they could go lol!

We were then stopped by a couple of interviewers from Calendar who were at Elland Road due to the death of Paul Madeley yesterday. Paul was an integral part of the great Don Revie side and part of the best-ever team that I was privileged to have seen. He signed a blank contract as he only wanted to play for Leeds; sadly, they don't make players like him anymore. RIP Tank and thank you for the memories.

We had a stop at a club in Bicester before getting to the ground at 7pm. It was weird seeing only three stands built at the moment, which I assumed was due to financial restraints but may be wrong on that score. There were a sizeable number of Leeds fans there for this pre-season friendly, which was good to see. I put my flag on display at the bottom of the stand. As I tried to shake the flag out I inadvertently caught my camera case, threw it over my head and knocked my beret off in the process. A big thank you to the Leeds fan (he said he'd touched the great flag) and the steward for helping me put the flag up. There is no hope for me but luckily the camera still worked thank goodness. That would have been catastrophic for me because, as well as the Leeds games, I have a

five-day trip to Berlin with my granddaughter Hannah in between the games to look forward to.

As usual I was talking to lots of people downstairs and it was good to see the Hampshire Whites. I then saw Collar and Tony, who I'd missed at the Forest Green game so managed to see them and have a chat. It was good to catch up with them and reminisce about Tony's Leeds United painted Capri car. The troubles he encountered in the past through parking it outside Supporters' Clubs or in car parks at away games was quite funny, although they weren't at the time. Because we were talking so much we missed the teams coming out so I was late getting photos of the Leeds mascot and the junior football team of one of our Oxford Whites. Luckily, I got some photos of the mascot in the centre of the pitch and the team in the stand opposite. Today also saw Radrizzani was back at a game and as many fans are getting increasingly worried about our lack of transfer activity, sadly it has seen a lot of nastiness on social media. Personally, I haven't given up hope as yet as there is still time with the transfer window and the loan window open until the end of August. There is still time until the fat lady sings (so the saying goes); once the windows are shut, that's when we will see what our ambitions as a club are.

The team: Will Huffer, Tom Pearce, Hugo Diaz, Mateusz Klich, Jamie Shackleton, Ronaldo Vieira, Yosuke Ideguchi, Lewis Baker, Sam Dalby, Oriol Rey and Jack Clarke. Subs: Jamal Blackman (making his debut after his season-long loan from Chelsea) for Huffer (45), Tyler Roberts for Ideguchi (45) and Ryan Edmondson for Dalby (45). Leeds lost 4-3 with goals from Roberts (54), Baker (63) and Clarke (71). Attendance was 4,772, including 1,335 Leeds fans. Leeds were to wear black armbands for Paul Madeley today, but it looked like Oxford were the only ones wearing them, which was sad really.

The team today was made up of lots of our youngsters; sadly, the first half was over before it began as Oxford scored on six minutes after Pearce, chasing his own pass, was unable to get to the ball first, resulting in Oxford taking the lead. They were two-up very soon, with a third goal before half-time. Booed off the pitch by some fans, we looked down and out.

As we went downstairs at half-time we heard that they had run out of food and it would be 15 minutes after half-time before there would be anymore. Apparently Oxford had panicked after hearing thousands of Leeds fans were coming to the game and sent for our stewards to attend.

Luckily for us, our subs at the start of the second half saw a tale of two halves and I really enjoyed it, and we also saw a goal glut. Roberts scored in the 54th minute but then Oxford scored a goal that was marginally offside but was given. If we thought Leeds were down and out we were mistaken, as Shackleton crossed for Baker to score. When Edmondson put the ball into the net for our third goal, this was disallowed for offside. Replays later showed this shouldn't have been disallowed. When Clarke scored what would have been our fourth goal, the correct score should have been 4-3 to us and not the other way around. I wasn't too despondent at the end of the game, though, because we had played well in the second half plus we showed we could score goals, which are always a plus sign.

I was glad I wasn't at work the next day as we got back to Leeds late. By the time I dropped Dani off at her house, it was 4am when I got back to mine. Our next game is Guiseley on Thursday so it feels like I've had no time in between games but see you there.

GUISELEY (A) – 26 JULY 2018

I picked my daughter Dani up and we headed straight to Elland Road to see my Bremner stone. Norman Hunter, Eddie Gray and Peter Lorimer had the honour of opening the square and when I saw the videos of this, I realised Norman (I think he was the one as I can't find the video now) was standing more or less on my stone. We found my stone in a prominent position in front of Billy and I am so happy. A big thank you to my family once again for getting me this present for Christmas. We hadn't been there long before it started spitting with rain. Dani decided she was going back to the car as I carried on looking around thinking a bit of rain won't harm me! Well that thought changed very quickly as the heavens opened with a torrential downpour. With that I headed back to the car to join Dani and we decided to go straight to Guiseley to avoid rush-hour traffic.

We were there very early but parked up, headed back to the Station pub and then sat outside with some other fans who we knew. It was very hot, we had a real laugh and they were great company. When we heard a massive crack of thunder I got very nervous but the storm stayed in the distance and it didn't rain. We headed back to the ground and I was going to get my Leeds United umbrella out of the car but weather forecasts were conflicting, with one saying more storms and another none at

all. We decided to go with the latter and stand outside the stand waiting for the team coach to arrive. It was nice to catch up with Dave (Les Cocker's son) along with his son Lee and grandson. Getting a photo of three generations of a Leeds legend was humbling and I'm glad I was able to do this.

I hung my flag up next to the players' tunnel and then we decided to stay where we were rather than go to sit down in the stand to the left of us. That turned out to be a big mistake because just as kick-off approached, the thunder cracked in the distance once more but the torrential rain came. As the rain bounced off the dry terraces we found our feet covered in dirt once it stopped. We felt sorry for the football teams and dance team who were all lined up on the pitch ready for the guard of honour, but they were troopers despite being soaked through.

The team: Blackman, Shackleton, De Bock, Diaz, Pearce, Klich, Vieira, Clarke, Baker, Roberts and Edmondson. Subs: Stevens for Roberts (38), Rey for Diaz (68) and Dalby for Edmondson (72). Attendance was a sell-out of 3,366, with Leeds and Guiseley fans mixing all over the ground.

Once again we found ourselves a goal down after three minutes then two goals down after 29. I thought here we go again but I remembered last year when Guiseley had taken a lead that we got back into the game. When Klich scored just before half-time at least we had that chance. Clarke brought us level four minutes into the second half, then Edmondson scored twice before Guiseley pulled one back but we won the game 4-3. At the end of the game there was a pitch invasion as loads of young kids ran onto the pitch to see the players. The young lad next to us was man handled by a female steward and pushed back over the fence. When there were loads of others already on the pitch it seemed over the top. Some of the players engaged well with the pitch invaders and took a long time to come off the pitch but it was good to see. The female steward then threw a group of Leeds youths out of the ground as they sang 'We'll never be mastered, by no Guiseley b*****ds' saying you can't do that here. Apparently she had been man handling a lot of the kids and angered some of our fans. It was a friendly after all!

We called at my nephew's house nearby after the game and then I headed home to Halifax via Wakefield as I'm a good mum! Our last pre-season game takes place at Elland Road on Sunday against Las Palmas before the season starts for real with our game against Stoke. There seems to be some transfer dealings going on in the background and indeed they have, as today, 28 July, the transfer of Barry Douglas (left-back) from Wolves has just been announced. I look forward to catching up with old and new friends so see you there.

LAS PALMAS (H) – 29 JULY 2018

It was a family affair today as I brought two of my daughters, Michelle and Dani, plus my three granddaughters, Hannah, Laura and Alexis, to the game. We had decided to go in early to the game and call at the White Rose beforehand as we thought it would be easier for the girls to get their dinner at McDonalds. It turned out that the White Rose was shut due to an evacuation test that had gone wrong so we ended up at Birstall instead.

After a trip to the Peacock we went into the ground and for once all our tickets were in the same stand as Michelle, Laura and Alexis were right at the front of the Kop whilst Dani, Hannah and I went to our normal places. I hadn't been able to buy one of our season ticket seats as it said online that it had been bought by family and friends. It turned out to be an empty seat so I reckon there must have been a blip on the system.

The team: Peacock-Farrell, Ayling, Berardi, Cooper, Dallas, Phillips, Vieira, Alioski, Saiz, Hernandez, and Roofe. Subs: Baker for Vieira (45), Klich for Saiz (45), Roberts for Alioski (64) and Shackleton subbing substitute Baker (88). Subs not used: Blackman, Huffer, Pearce and Clarke. Leeds won 1-0, with Roofe scoring the goal (86). Attendance was 11,499 with approximately 30-50 Las Palmas fans. This turned out to be Vieira's last game for us as he was transferred to Sampdoria two days later.

The first half saw Las Palmas hit the crossbar twice as both sides had chances but we went in at half-time with no goals scored. The second half saw Hernandez unlucky not to score when his shot was saved by their goalkeeper. There hadn't been too much goalmouth action but Leeds took the lead with a goal from Roofe with four minutes of normal time left on the clock.

With the last game of the pre-season friendlies over, next Sunday sees the first game of the season with our home game against relegated Stoke. In the meantime, I will be having a short break in Berlin with my granddaughter Hannah and will be flying the flag for Leeds by wearing our Leeds shirts on the journey.

Heidi and Hannah,
Brandenburger Tor, Berlin

CHAPTER 2

STOKE CITY (H) – 5 AUGUST 2018

Having been in Berlin with intermittent Wi-Fi, I missed a lot of what happened at Elland Road over the last week. Seeing that Vieira was sold to Sampdoria was a shock and not something I expected now the season was ready to start. I'd seen comments previously on one of the groups on social media saying that he hadn't impressed over the pre-season games; I only hope there are future clauses added to ensure we don't miss out cash wise if he achieves his potential. We also signed Jack Harrison, a winger from Manchester City, on a season-long loan and Patrick Bamford, a centre-forward from Middlesbrough. Also, Sacko went on a season-long loan to Las Palmas. I also found out that I'd made an appearance in the Sky documentary about Leeds that had been shown on Thursday, *Leading Leeds United*. I was there with my camera at Bootham Crescent at the York pre-season game taking a video as Bielsa came off the coach. He was smiling at me and touched my shoulder and if I remember right it was because I got in the way and said sorry. I got a message from my son Jamie today asking if I was always on the TV. It was still a proud moment to see that I had been included in this though. As always I will share my love of Leeds United around the world through my books, blogs and photos.

This game had already changed to a Sunday with a 4.30pm kick-off for a live Sky game, but it hadn't deterred the Leeds United faithful with a crowd of over 34,000 expected. Included in the total

Heidi and Hannah leaving Stockport International airport

were the Stoke fans who had sold out their own allocation. There was to be a tribute in the South Stand to Paul Madeley, applause before the game for him, and fans had been asked to wear white.

It was good to be back at Elland Road for the first game of the season, despite being there a week ago for the friendly against Las Palmas. There was a real buzz about the place as I headed to the Peacock with my daughter Danielle and granddaughter Laura. When I'd picked Danielle up earlier we got stuck in diversions and road closures in Dewsbury and I was glad it was still a few hours to kick-off. At one point I thought we'd never get out of there as every road we tried was closed but thank goodness we got out in the end.

Can I say a big thank you to a young lady, who will remain nameless at this moment in time, for buying all four of my books which will be a present. As always, your support is appreciated. I was hoping my fifth book *Back to Reality with Leeds United, 2017-18* would be out but I am still awaiting confirmation from my publisher.

It was great to see that many of our Norwegian supporters were over for the game. Sadly I was still travelling back from Berlin so missed their get together on Friday evening. There were also some of our Irish supporters here too. On my trip to Berlin with my granddaughter Hannah, we went to the Brandenburger Tor as soon as we arrived, having worn our Leeds United shirts whilst travelling. This had to be done especially when flying from 'Stockport International Airport!' I was just about to take a selfie when a lad came up to us and asked if we wanted another Leeds fan to take it for us; of course was the answer. He was a Leeds United fan from South Africa and by wearing our colours everywhere this does encourage others to talk to you. Once again this shows to me how much we have a fantastic worldwide fan base.

The Peacock was very busy and the garden was packed. With the sun shining and that 'perfect' football weather, there were plenty of high spirits and optimism in the air. Personally I was looking forward to the season with a positive outlook. You've got to be that way as far as I'm concerned at

the start of the season but as always the proof will be on the pitch. I know many fans haven't felt this way at all but I like to see for myself how things pan out and will always give things a chance. I realised there was no hope for me as I went to get my camera out of the case and it wasn't there. I was going to take a photo of some fans and just as I was panicking, they pointed out that my camera was attached to my wrist. I'd already taken some photos before that, hence why the case was empty.

We went into the ground in good time in readiness for the start. The stands all looked great, with loads of white shirts everywhere and it felt like there was going to be a great atmosphere. One thing I will say is despite the 50+ number of years I have followed Leeds United, there were still plenty of faces that I didn't recognise today. In the 70s and 80s you would have a large hardcore of fans who went everywhere and even if I didn't know their names, I would always recognise their faces. Now, with our fan base being bigger than ever, it isn't surprising that I don't know everyone anymore.

After the applause and the cards in the South Stand (Eleven Pauls) the game was ready to start. It was also good to see Paul's teammates from the Revie era applauding from the touchline too. One thing I was hoping for was that our fitness levels would be the best they have been for years under Bielsa's training.

The team: Bailey Peacock-Farrell, Luke Ayling, Kalvin Phillips, Samuel Saiz, Barry Douglas (making his debut at left-back), Liam Cooper, Gaetano Berardi, Ezgjan Alioski, Pablo Hernandez, Mateusz Klich and Kemar Roofe. Subs: Stuart Dallas for Klich (76), Lewis Baker for Saiz (88) and Jack Harrison for Alioski (89). Leeds won the game 3-1, with Klich (15), Hernandez (45 + 1) and Cooper (57) scoring for Leeds. Stoke scored with a penalty (52) by Afobe. The attendance was 34,126, with 2,471 Stoke fans.

The game set off with a great pace against Stoke City, who had been relegated from the Premier League at the end of last season. We had plenty of possession and our passing was good as the team were collectively fighting for every ball. We had an early chance after Alioski sent over a cross and Roofe's volley was saved by Butland in the nets for Stoke. (The Leeds fans made Butland laugh in the second half when he was in front of the Kop. They sang he was a s**t Jordan Pickford – England's goalkeeper – and he started clapping and laughed.) That made the Leeds fans sing Butland is a Leeds fan. It wasn't long before Leeds took the lead though after Saiz kept hold of the ball and passed it to Klich, who ran forward into the penalty area to put the ball into the net – 1-0 as the celebrating Leeds fans went berserk on the terraces. We had a good chance to go two-up before Ince (getting loads of abuse from the Leeds fans because his dad played for man u) hit the crossbar for Stoke. We were playing some good football with precise passing between our players. Alioski brought another save out of Butland which prevented us getting a second goal. There was always a danger that Stoke could get back into the game and I wanted another goal to give us a cushion. This was provided when Hernandez sent a shot into the left-hand corner of the goal in front of the South Stand. I was poised to see the goal go into the net and ready to take a photo of the action, only for Danielle to knock my elbow as the ball went in as she celebrated us scoring. It felt good to be two goals up as we went in at half-time.

After joining Carole, Ashley, Margaret and Keith at half-time, we had to disappoint a Leeds fan as we weren't taking bets. We have taken to standing behind the betting area beneath the stands and it does raise a laugh. The conversation was very positive about the way we were playing and long may it continue.

After attacking initially at the start of the second half it was very disappointing when the ref pointed to the spot, giving Stoke a penalty. I was hoping they would miss it but unfortunately Peacock-Farrell went the wrong way. Here we go again, especially as the ref seemed to have a brain exchange at half-time, in my opinion. We were being picked up for fouls and he was letting those on us go so nothing had changed in that respect. For once it didn't stop us and before long we won a corner, and as Douglas sent the ball into the centre, Cooper was on hand to head it into the net for our third goal of the day. The celebrating Leeds fans couldn't believe it but it was good to see that we were scoring goals too. We didn't have it all our own way, though, as in the second half Stoke came close on a couple of occasions. When Peter Crouch came on I couldn't believe he was still playing as he seems to have been around for ages. He is still a giant, though, and caused our defence some problems, but luckily for us we were able to keep them out and get the season off to a great start with a win and three points.

It was great to see everyone, including the subs and those not used, come onto the pitch to clap the fans at the end of the game. Although Bielsa failed to confirm this had happened, he had the players picking up litter for three hours so they could appreciate how long fans have to work to watch them play. All I want to see from a team is them giving their all, fighting for the ball and, even if they lose it, getting it back as soon as possible. What Bielsa has done with the team on today's showing is exactly that and that is all I ask for. We are in for an exciting season and I am positive that will happen because whatever happens next, they are going to play for the shirt and put the commitment in that the fans do. Even Pontus Jansson, despite being an unused sub, went to the South Stand at the end and interacted with them again. That is something he stopped doing early last season and I could never understand why.

We headed into the club shop to see how the refurbishment had gone. To hear that the new shirt was only available in an XL shirt, having sold out of the rest, just shows how replica shirts and memorabilia for Leeds fans are high on the agenda. Once in the car I made the mistake of heading towards Elland Road to go up Wesley Street. I've no idea what was going on but all of a sudden there were three police vans parked across Elland Road with flashing lights and sirens going off. They were getting ready to escort the Stoke buses out but I wasn't sure if they had fans who had travelled by train or not. Someone will know what happened and will put us in the picture, no doubt.

After dropping Danielle off, Laura and I headed to Rastrick to pick up one of my other granddaughters, Hannah, before eventually getting home at 10pm. Once again it has taken a while to write this blog up (as usual falling asleep) so I will post onto my *Follow Me and Leeds United* page and my own page and then share amongst the groups in the morning. Please feel free to share the blog with any other Leeds fans/Leeds groups on social media that you know would be interested to read it.

Next week sees us travel to Derby on my birthday for another late kick-off of 5.30pm. A great present would be another win, so fingers crossed.

DERBY (A) – 11 AUGUST 2018

Good news for me, I have now proofread my latest book *Back to Reality, Leeds United 2017-18* and sent this back to my publisher. Fingers crossed it will be out in the next few weeks. I have approximately 200 photos (including collages) from our journey to games last season in the book as it is written as a fan for the fans. I will have a quota to sell and I am hopeful that it will be available in the club shop but will keep you informed.

A big thank you to everyone who took time to wish/sing a happy birthday to me today, plus the special card I received from the Leeds United stewards, it was all appreciated. As for the best birthday present I could have asked for, take a bow Marcelo Bielsa and Leeds United. I asked for a win and three points and that performance today was out of this world! Commiserations to my publisher Steve though as his birthday wishes only lasted until 5.30pm. Somehow I think I got the better deal lol!

As the game was being shown live on Sky with a 5.30pm kick-off, the coach was leaving Leeds at

1.30pm. Billy's bar was open for us too, which was good to see. My friend Sue was travelling by car to the game with her husband Paul as they were coming from the opposite direction. My daughter Danielle (Dani) was picked up with some others at Junction 39 before we headed to Chesterfield for our pub stop. We had a nice break before arriving at the ground at 4.50pm. It was nice to catch up with many fans before the game and there was quite a queue outside the turnstiles. I thought Dani was to go in through a different entrance to me, but she came back to inform me that I'd been looking on the ticket at the area inside the ground. Oops, at least I hadn't gone looking for it! I then tried trapping my arm in the turnstile but I soon moved it out of the way as it began to hurt!

After putting my flag up I headed up to my seat and once again found our away season tickets were right at the top of the stand. As I found my seat next to the home fans, I wondered why we were put up in the Gods and so far from the pitch. I was around lots I knew though and sat next to Whitby John again.

The team: Peacock-Farrell, Berardi, Ayling, Cooper, Phillips, Saiz, Alioski, Douglas, Roofe, Klich and Hernandez. Subs: Jamie Shackleton for Klich (73), Patrick Bamford for Roofe (79) and Lewis Baker for Saiz (86). Leeds won the game 4-1, with goals from Klich (5), Roofe (21 and 60) and Alioski (64). Attendance was 27,311, with 2,000 Leeds fans.

One of my friends tweeted that it would be a draw but I said I wanted a win and three points. At that time, I would never have believed that I would get my wish in such style though. My concerns last season were that we weren't fit enough and as Bielsa has rectified that I looked forward to seeing the difference it made. I also enjoyed seeing the team playing as one, backing each other up and getting the win against Stoke last week. I'm definitely looking forward to the Bielsa effect.

Derby had limited the amount of tickets we got for this game and they'd all sold out as usual. There were lads who'd come to the game without tickets but found there weren't any spares to be had. Underneath the stands the fans were in fine voice, singing about Douglas. Bielsa had named the same team as last week as Leeds got off to a dream start. Within five minutes we were one goal up when Klich sent a great strike from the edge of the box into the Derby goal. The team headed to our corner to celebrate with the Leeds fans, who were ecstatic. Some Derby fans to the right of us started to cause issues with some of our fans. At first I thought there had just been some banter but I think they were making personal comments. At first the Derby stewards were having a go at the Leeds fans for retaliating, but after complaints by some of our fans, one of our stewards came and stood there too. One of the younger stewards was a Leeds fan as he'd been talking to Whitby John before the game kicked off.

The ref let a few tackles on us go without giving a free kick but was quick off the mark to give Derby one. Unfortunately, they drew level from this free kick with a fantastic shot that beat Peacock-Farrell, although he didn't stand a chance with it. Of course the celebrating Derby fans woke up very quickly then. To get an atmosphere going they have a drummer behind the goal facing their fans, but he wasn't even watching the game which I found weird. The good thing

though was that Leeds carried on where they left off. We were playing as a team, battling, fighting for each other, using simple passes and then fantastic crosses to the other side of the pitch. It was good to see, especially when Alioski crossed the ball into the middle for Roofe to jump above everyone to head the ball into the net to put us back into the lead. We played some really good stuff and were unlucky not to get another goal. Derby hadn't given up though so I was glad to get to half-time still in the lead.

At the start of the second half we looked very jittery for a few minutes as we started making a few mistakes. I just hoped this wouldn't give Derby the impetus to take the game by the scruff of the neck. I needn't have worried because we got going again and extended our lead, with Roofe scoring his second goal of the game after Klich's great pass to him. Even better still, we got a fourth when Alioski headed the ball into the net after great work from Hernandez. Unbelievable scenes of celebrations from the Leeds fans as I don't think we could actually believe we had scored four goals at Pride Park. Having been a bogey ground for us for many years, it was a fantastic feeling to know that we were playing some fantastic football as well as winning. When Shackleton came on as sub in place of Klich, he was unfazed and I knew that Bielsa had worked with the youngsters too so they would slot into place. At York he had played on the wing but he was brought on more into the middle of the pitch. With one Derby attack when Peacock-Farrell indicated the Derby player had stamped on his foot, Shackleton went to help him. I was impressed with the fight he put up against the Derby player to ensure he didn't get a free shot at our goal.

The Leeds fans had been in good voice throughout the game and it was a feeling of immense pride when the final whistle blew and we had won in style. I had already gone down to the front to get my flag and had taken photos of lots I knew and many were shouting for me to take their photos. Jansson came over at the end of the game to interact with the fans and he threw his brand new away shirt into the crowd, which was caught and handed to one of our disabled fans. He was wearing it on the way out of the ground so I was able to get photos and he was chuffed to bits and well done.

I met Dani and Sue at the end of the game and then we headed back to the coach. After a police escort away from the ground we were back on the M1 in no time. After dropping Dani and others off in the rain, we got to Elland Road and it was only spitting. I gave Roy a lift home as his car was poorly, before getting home in good time.

Tuesday sees our Carabao Cup game against Bolton at Elland Road before we take on Rotherham in the league next week. The cup game will see those who haven't played already getting a game. I won't make predictions, but, although things have started off similar to the last couple of seasons, there is a difference to the team on view.

We will have made the other teams in the division sit up and take notice, especially as both games have been live on Sky so far. Let's enjoy the ride and for once it would be nice to have more ups than downs.

BOLTON (H), CARABAO CUP FIRST ROUND – 14 AUGUST 2018

As my granddaughter Hannah and I arrived at the ground our first stop was the club shop. I'd met my publisher Steve unexpectedly yesterday and he said that three of my books were on sale in the shop, which was good to hear. The book area had been delayed as the sale of the home shirts had taken over from sorting out more of the layout. It looked really good in there today and there is lots of memorabilia for sale now. From there we went to the Peacock and met my daughter Dani and friends Sue and Keith. As we walked into the pub a lad from Halifax came over to say hello and I remembered the name Bukit immediately. As he keeps up to date with my blog in Spain, it was nice to say hello. After taking a couple of photos we headed into the ground as there were going to be queues at the turnstiles, as the sales of tickets had gone through the roof in the last few days. The Bielsa effect is obviously having an impact and whetted the appetite of fans for this cup tie even though there were going to be a lot of changes to the team. On our way there someone came up to me to ask if there are any Leeds fans out there who didn't know it was my birthday last Saturday. Obviously he'd seen all the messages I received on Facebook etc.

The team: Blackman, Shackleton, Ayling, Jansson, Baker, Harrison, Bamford, Phillips, Roberts, Saiz and Pearce. A double substitution of Klich for Roberts and Alioski for Saiz (68) then Roofe for Bamford (80) took place. Leeds won the game 2-1, with goals by Bamford (27) and Saiz (35). Attendance was 19,617, with 1,007 Bolton fans.

With the wholesale changes to the team, I didn't feel like I normally do – apprehensive – because as far as I can see, Bielsa will be getting every player at the club to play the same way. This means to me that they would be able to slot into any position they were asked to play. The first half an hour saw Leeds have plenty of possession and saw a couple of early chances. Phillips looked like he was the engine room and had a good game. Jamie Shackleton was making his home debut and I do like the lad. Seeing him give as good as he got when protecting Blackman in goal made me laugh, but it was impressive. He is going to be a good one for the future that's for sure. All of a sudden Bamford got the ball in an attack, got past one Bolton player before putting the ball into the net for a debut goal. Eight minutes later we got a second goal when Saiz scored after some great footwork and we broke out of defence into an attack. At that time we looked like we would be comfortable winners.

The second half saw Bolton come out on the attack and our play wasn't as fluent as it had been in the first half. It wasn't a surprise when they pulled one back and could so easily have equalised before we got back into the game. Both Harrison and Shackleton put some great crosses in but we were unable to do anything with it. The young lad behind me was concerned that we had eight men in attack near the end of the game. I said it was because we won't sit on a one-goal lead anymore and whilst he understood that, I don't think he understood the Bielsa concept. My motto of the best form of defence is attack means that I am happy with what Bielsa is bringing to the squad as a whole. There was some rustiness amongst a few of the players in the team today and some frustrations amongst them when things didn't come off. With having no reserve teams of old to get playing time, and despite having a smaller squad, it looks like the players on the edge of the first team will be used in the cup games. Whilst I'm not a lover of a weakened team for cup games, for once it didn't feel like it due to the fact that Bielsa wants everyone to play the same way. What I did like to see was the trainers all getting involved at the side of the pitch and sending instructions to the players. Bielsa also didn't stay perched on his bucket but would get up to have a word with them too. After both Monk and Heckingbottom stood at the side with folded arms, I found that a breath of fresh air.

Just before the end of the game some lads behind tried singing Wembley, Wembley, we're the famous Leeds United and we're off to Wembley. I just thought no please wait with that song as I didn't want it jinxing the game. With many of our fans in the East Stand heading for the exits, I thought they must be confident that Bolton won't get an equaliser and weren't waiting for extra time. To be honest, on that basis I'm assuming that nothing has changed with the rules for cup games since last season though. I did get a bit jittery in those last few minutes, but we ended the game with a win and through to the next round. We'll know soon enough who our next opponents will be; if it's away I would like to have a new ground to visit.

I would like to say a big thank you to Pete for buying my book *Follow Me and Leeds United* which is appreciated; enjoy the read. Also thanks for the feedback from everyone who enjoys reading my blog.

Saturday sees Rotherham come to Elland Road for the second home game in a week, and we will be looking at a near-sell-out crowd. I feel that Bielsa will stick with the same team as the one that played against Derby unless there are any injuries.

ROTHERHAM (H) – 18 AUGUST 2018

On our way to Elland Road we heard that the game was now a sell-out from a Leeds fan's perspective, with the only tickets available being in the Rotherham area. After a quick trip to the White Rose we got to the ground at 1.15pm, the earliest for a long while, as I was meeting my sister Erica and also Simon was here from Cornwall. As Dani, Laura and I headed to the Peacock, Erica and Paul, her friend, caught up with us at the traffic lights. It was nice to catch up with lots of fans in the Peacock and Beano, who goes in the South Stand, was trying to get a new song going about Bielsa and his bucket! As we headed into the ground Laura wanted to go via my Bremner stone, but I was disgusted to see that someone had spilt their chips and tomato sauce over the steps to Billy's statue. This is sacred ground to me and I couldn't for the life of me understand why anyone would treat the area in any other way. It had been cleared away when we got there after the game, although there were stains where the food had been.

The team: Peacock-Farrell, Ayling, Berardi, Cooper, Phillips, Saiz, Alioski, Roofe, Hernandez, Douglas and Klich. Subs: Baker for Saiz (80), Bamford for Roofe (86) and Jansson for Klich (90).

Follow Me
& Leeds United

Heidi Haigh

Leeds won the game 2-0, with Luke Ayling scoring his first league goal (49) and Roofe getting the other (72). Attendance was 33,699, with 707 Rotherham fans.

The first 20 minutes saw Leeds have a couple of chances, but with Rotherham shooting on sight they were unlucky not to score first. With one bad pass from Cooper to Peacock-Farrell, it looked odds-on that Rotherham were going to score, but they had the ball whipped off their toes to deny them a goal. They also had a long-range shot hit the post as they were taking the game to Leeds. At this time our players were a bit jittery, seemingly to me because

Daily Express 1975 — front cover Follow Me and Leeds United showing Carole with same scarf as above.

51

of the full house spurring them on. I felt they needed a goal to calm those nerves but we were playing out from the back and kept passing the ball back to Peacock-Farrell, which was too close for comfort at times. Before half-time we came close with a fantastic shot from Klich that just went at the wrong side of the upright and their goalie saved a great attempt by Berardi.

Laura and I met up with Carole, Ashley, Margaret and Keith behind the betting desk as usual. Carole was wearing her scarf from the 70s and I still love this piece of history and it makes me wish I hadn't got rid of lots of my things. I did get the chance to buy one of my scarves back on eBay recently but someone beat me to it at the last minute. I recognised it straight away because as well as the patches it had a familiar ladder at the front of it where I'd worn a pin badge.

Whatever Bielsa said to the team at half-time it worked, as the team came out on fire for the second half. Within four minutes we had taken the lead when Douglas's corner caused havoc in the Rotherham goalmouth. With Cooper's header saved by the goalie, Roofe passed the rebound back across and Ayling's header crossed the line despite the Rotherham player's attempt to clear it. As Ayling wasn't sure whether to celebrate, he looked to the referee and as the goal was given he ran exuberantly to the East Stand. As this was his first league goal, I'm not surprised. This goal took the heat off the team and some of the passing in this half was out of this world. With Saiz jinking past players as if the ball was attached to his feet by a rope, our attacking just got better and better and he was unlucky not to score when his effort was headed off the line. Coming out from defence into attack saw Roofe get a second goal for us; Phillips sent a pin-point pass over the defence for Roofe to run on to along the front of the West Stand. Roofe beat their man at the edge of the box and then, from a narrow angle, put the ball into the net to send the Leeds fans into fantastic celebrations. When *Super Leeds* and *Marching on Together* were sung in the Kop and most of the ground it was spine tingling and it felt like a very special moment. Hearing *Super Leeds* ringing out from the stands like it did, this felt like a momentous occasion as I can't remember it sung like this for a long, long time. Apart from Peacock-Farrell making a great save in the last few minutes, we were able to see the game out comfortably in our favour.

I think out fitness levels overcame Rotherham today as well as having a positive mental attitude and fighting for every ball. There were mistakes made, especially in the first half, but in the past we would have lost these challenges and the mistakes would have been costly. By chasing down everything, this enabled us to get on top of the game. Bielsa's impact on this cannot be underestimated either. The fact that Bielsa is the first Leeds United manager (I don't do coaches, sorry!) to have won his first four games in charge is another milestone. Listening to his interview on BBC Radio Leeds on the way home makes me like him even more. It is not about him but the team and he looks at what isn't working and tries to rectify it. He is a man of my heart because he has got the team fighting for everything and never giving up, which is something I always wanted to see my team do. Let's enjoy the moment Leeds fans because it is about time our long-suffering support has something positive and exciting to watch on the field.

Tuesday sees us head to Swansea for the first of two away games in a row with a 9.30am departure from Leeds before we head to Norwich on Saturday. I'm looking forward to enjoying two away games with our fans but also looking forward to seeing what we produce on the pitch.

SWANSEA (A) – 21 AUGUST 2018

The coach was leaving Leeds at 9.30am today and I got there in plenty time. After a quick look at some of the Bremner Stones, with pick-ups at Wakefield, Chesterfield and Tamworth, we headed to Porthcawl for our pub stop. After sunshine most of the way down, it started raining but luckily it stopped by the time we got off the coach. I made sure we got a photo of a group of us at the sea front as soon as we got off the coach and posted it straight away on Twitter and Facebook (unfortunately we couldn't go onto the beach as it was cordoned off). The story of Leeds fans everywhere continued as the chap I asked to take a photo of us turned out to be a Leeds fan, although he was not wearing his Strongbow shirt! At the pub we sat outside enjoying the sunshine, when the chap who took our photo for us pulled up on the road next to us and shouted to us. His grandchildren didn't look too impressed though! Martin made us laugh when he started talking to the lad next to him on the coach about a book he was mentioned in and found out he was the writer of it! It's a small world.

We had a lovely three-hour stop with good company, lots of laughs and something to eat and drink. We got to the ground around 7pm and it was a shock to see two armed police standing there before we entered the compound. I was surprised to see them and also that the away area was cordoned off. There again, they were making sure we didn't have a repetition of the last time we were there, when some windows on the buses back to the station were put through. When we had played Swansea at Elland Road in the same season, there were many Swansea fans who via the internet said they also liked Leeds. I'd been standing at Billy's statue when a lad approached me asking if I could take a photo of him with Billy, which I did. Unfortunately there were some younger Leeds fans who took exception to the Swansea fans and I'm positive that's why we saw the issues on our last visit sadly.

We got into the ground relatively quickly and there were a lively bunch of Leeds fans under the stand. Thanks to all the fans who wanted their photos taken today, and there were a lot that's for sure. As two fans have requested purchasing all five of my books (the fifth is due out shortly), I will have to ensure I replenish my stock of a couple of them in readiness. My daughter Dani and I went to the top of the stand to hang my flag up and it was great to see so many flags today. What had been quite funny was us two saying goodbye outside the stand; we thought we were going in different entrances with Dani's seat being in the bottom whilst mine was in the top half. We found out inside that we were able to get anywhere in the stand after all.

After Bielsa had named an unchanged squad, it surprised me when I saw Shackleton on the pitch. Only then did I find out that Cooper had injured himself in the pre-game warm up and had

a hamstring injury. We could have done with his height that's for sure as Swansea had some 'brick s***houses' playing for them.

The team: Peacock-Farrell, Ayling, Berardi, Roofe, Hernandez, Saiz, Alioski, Shackleton (making his full debut), Klich, Phillips and Douglas. Subs: Baker for Phillips (28), Harrison for Alioski (45) and Bamford for Roofe (64). Score was 2-2, with Roofe (40) and Hernandez (79) scoring for Leeds. Attendance was 20,860, with approximately 2,100 Leeds fans who had sold out their allocation in minutes – excellent support once again, despite this being a mid-week game and live on Sky. Leeds came back from behind twice to get a well-earned point and went top of the league tonight (although there are other clubs playing tomorrow so that may change).

As the game kicked off we found ourselves up against a tough team (they'd obviously been watching us). The ref, A. Davies, showed his true colours immediately and continued this for the whole game, booking our players and falling for every challenge, giving free kicks galore. Their number nine should have been booked for a blatant dive in the penalty area, despite our player already running away with the ball he'd won when the player went down. The same player went nuts at the linesman when he flagged for a foul and the fact he got away with it didn't go down well with the Leeds fans. He continued to rant and nothing was even said to him, unbelievable! Swansea took the play to us with constant attacking and not giving us a chance to settle. After Phillips was robbed of the ball, Swansea continued with the attack and we found ourselves a goal down sadly; although Peacock-Farrell got his hands to the ball, he was unable to save it going into the net. It wasn't surprising really, although a little disappointing, but I knew we were up against it. Bielsa made an immediate change, taking off Phillips and bringing on Baker. We had been struggling to stop Swansea attacking and it was a bold move from Bielsa. As this was the first game this season that we had gone behind, it would be interesting to see how we would react as a team. Well the team didn't disappoint; we managed to get an attack on their goal and it was great to see Roofe put the ball into the net to equalise after great work from Shackleton on the right. This was the half-time score and at least we were still in the game.

At half-time I went to look for Tony from the West Midlands as Billy was looking for him. I used to travel with Billy's dad's coaches to away games in the 70s and Tony used to stay at their house. It was good to catch up with both of them. When we discussed how long ago we had met, it was unbelievable really as Tony hasn't aged at all. Scunny was there too and I got more requests for photos so was happy to oblige. Tony said before the game today he'd gone into a pub near the ground with his Leeds shirt on and this man shouted out, 'I remember you from 1981 as you were the only black person to come into the pub then!'

As the second half kicked off, and with the Leeds fans in good voice, Bielsa made a further change when Alioski was replaced by Harrison. I'd noticed Alioski had his right hand bandaged and when I mentioned it to Dave who stood next to me he said it had been like that on Saturday. I hadn't noticed it but then realised I'd not bothered putting my glasses on so no wonder! Things took a turn for the worse again as we found ourselves behind when they scored a second goal. Damn! I'd started to get butterflies in my stomach but I still hoped we could get something out of the game. Without looking at my photos (I hoped I'd captured the moment), when Bamford got past their player on the wing and passed the ball across to Hernandez in the penalty area I had my camera poised as there was no way he was missing that one. The equaliser sent the celebrating Leeds fans into raptures and at that time I felt we could go on and win the game. Shortly after Swansea were through on goal and it looked like they were going to get the winner, only for Peacock-Farrell to make a fantastic save with his feet to deny them. Leeds came into their own then as we found our feet and looked all on that we would get that winner, only for their player to go down 'injured', I mean time wasting in the penalty area. Still, as the final whistle blew and despite the draw meaning we'd dropped our first points of the season, the team got a fantastic reception from the Leeds fans. It was lovely to see George get Berardi's shirt at the end of the game too. George had been mascot, plus it was also his birthday, so he'd had a great day and a birthday to remember. It was Berardi's 30th birthday today too, plus Phillips (100) and Alioski (50) also reached milestones with games played. As I went to get my flag at the end of the game, someone helped me climb over the seats, only for cramp to start in my calf and feet again, ouch!

I know we didn't play too well at times today, but we showed character to come back from behind twice and get something from the game. At one time we would have capitulated and been beaten so I will take the positives from today. Bielsa definitely takes things seriously, seeing him getting up off the bucket and taking everything in about the game is good to see. The fact that he changed things quickly is also a breath of fresh air too.

Luckily I'm not in work in the morning but I know some people are so I feel for you. Personally, I got home at 4am with a 20-hour round trip behind me. The Liberty Stadium hasn't been a good hunting ground for us or Vetch field (Swansea's old ground) so I'm happy with a point. See you at Norwich on Saturday for another tough game.

NORWICH (A) – 25 AUGUST 2018

With an early start beckoning, what I didn't expect was to be wide awake for most of the night. With my Fitbit showing I had only one hour 21 minutes sleep, I felt like death warmed up. As I got to Leeds I realised why I'd been cold as the temperature was at a low eight degrees which is not something we've been used to of late. The good thing, though, was that the sky was blue and I got a fantastic photo of Billy's statue and the ground in glorious sunshine. Luckily for me I was able to sleep most of the way to our pub stop in Thetford, where LUSC Fullerton Park members raised a toast in remembrance of our two supporters, Paul Turner and Keith Horner, who both died during the close season and were regular travellers with the branch.

On arrival in Norwich at 2.15pm, we got straight in the ground and I went to the front of the stand to put my flag up near the corner, before taking some customary photos. I'd said to my

daughter Danielle that last season my flag got soaked due to the rain; I obviously tempted fate because the next thing the heavens opened but luckily it didn't last too long and the sun came back out again.

The team: Peacock-Farrell, Ayling, Berardi, Phillips, Hernandez, Douglas, Alioski, Saiz, Klich, Roofe and Jansson coming in for his first league game of the season after Cooper's injury. Forshaw and Dallas are also out due to injury. Subs: Bamford for Roofe (77), Harrison for Hernandez (79) and Baker for Saiz (90). Leeds won the game 3-0, with Klich (21), Alioski (26) and Hernandez (67) scoring the Leeds goals. Attendance was 25,944, with approximately 2,500 Leeds fans.

Norwich had painted the away changing rooms pink in an effort to unsettle us as a team, although the dug outs remained the same with the Leeds team warming up at the far end of the pitch. It took about 15 minutes for us to get a grip of the game as Norwich set out to attack us. The Leeds fans were in fine voice, despite there being no alcohol served in the ground. Once we got over the early pressure from Norwich, Leeds turned on a fantastic display of football, going two goals up in the first half. After Alioski's header was saved by their keeper, the ball came back out to Klich on the edge of the area and he hammered the ball past their goalie for our first goal. When Alioski got the second one the Leeds fans upped their singing even more, enjoying the display being put on by the team. Although Norwich threatened a few times, Leeds were playing as a team and fighting for everything, meaning we were able to nullify any threats as we went into the break in the lead. There were lots of smiling faces and happy Leeds fans, with many wanting their photos taken.

When our fans were singing we were top of the league and also Leeds are going up, I refused to sing it as I wasn't going to put a jinx on things. We were playing some great football and running rings around Norwich, who at times were chasing shadows. We're taking the p**s sang the gleeful Leeds support as Norwich, although they kept plugging away, were no match for us as we fought for everything. When Hernandez side-stepped their player in the penalty area, I knew the ball was going in as soon as it left his foot to put us three goals up and game over. At that time, unbeknown to me but near where Danielle was standing, the celebrating Leeds fans fell down the rows and the steps with many fans at the bottom of the pile including Norwich stewards. If ever there was an advert for safe standing this was it. Unfortunately someone we know was hurt in the melee and was taken to first aid with an injured back. Someone at the end of the game was being helped down the steps by two lads as he was limping badly with another celebration injury. Hopefully both of them and any others who were hurt will be okay.

At the end of the game all the players came over to the Leeds fans but there were so many stewards stood in front of us I couldn't get a clear view, but it was nice to see both Alioski and Jansson take off their shirts to hand to fans. I then noticed that young Jack, one of our loyal Welsh Whites, was the lucky recipient of Jansson's shirt. To be fair, though, the stewards had been very relaxed and happy for me to take photos of all the flags and many of our fans. I was also able to go and get my flag near the end of the game.

It was a very happy and satisfied support walking back to the coaches, that's for sure. As I mentioned numerous times in my blogs last year about our lack of fitness, it was a unanimous vote that our fitness levels this year under Bielsa are going to make a difference. Whatever is thrown at us, it will be exciting to watch I'm sure of that!

With Tuesday's game against Preston at Elland Road in the next round of the Carabao Cup, there will be a number of changes to the team, with those who haven't had any game time given the chance to shine. We then finish the week with Friday's second home game in a week against Middlesbrough. Bring it on and I'll see you there.

PRESTON (H), SECOND ROUND CARABAO CUP – 28 AUGUST 2018

What can I say but a big thank you to all those Leeds fans who have stood up to be counted and given me fantastic support for sharing my blogs. After receiving some abuse from someone about the fact my blog showed up in about ten different Facebook groups, the reaction I have had from other Leeds fans has been totally overwhelming.

After posting the following when sharing the blog the response has been phenomenal: 'As always I post my blog and photos for those fans who want to read them. If it isn't for you then

please ignore them but please do not resort to abuse as I received earlier tonight. I'm pleased to report that this has now been deleted by one of the groups I post in. I understand that some fans are in many groups the same as me so receive the same post many times. If anyone has any ideas how to manage my posts better I am happy to discuss these further because it does take a lot of time and effort to do this. If you do not want me to share in your group then please let me know. As I want to get the photos out to as many fans as possible and we do have a fantastic worldwide fan base, how do I do this if I don't share it? I am happy for Leeds fans to share the blogs themselves if that is easier but look forward to hearing your views. The rest of the blog and photos are on my website link below: http://www.followmeandleedsunited.co.uk/norwich-v-leeds-united-25th-august-2018-at-carrow-road'

My response to everyone for their support was: 'Due to an overwhelming response of gratitude for what I do, please note I will still be sharing my blog in all the Leeds United groups that I am in. If it isn't for you then please ignore and scroll past. Thank you. Marching on Together!' Leeds fans are one in a million that's for sure.

As we headed to Elland Road, there would be a lot of changes to the team today, but for once I wasn't worried about square pegs in round holes. As Bielsa is getting everyone to play the same way, this means that anyone stepping into the team should be able to play wherever he puts them. We arrived an hour before kick-off and went to the Peacock to meet friends before going into the ground. As we walked out of the Peacock it was nice to meet someone off the new forum I was asked to post in – www.not606.com. I didn't realise how close it was to kick-off once we were through the queues at the turnstiles so missed the teams coming out.

The team: Blackman, Phillips, Jansson, Shaughnessy, Harrison, Dallas, Baker, Roberts, Shackleton, Pearce and Bamford. Subs: Klich for Shaughnessy (45), Saiz for Shackleton (45) and Alioski for Roberts (60). Leeds lost the game 2-0, their first defeat of the season under Bielsa's management. Attendance was 18,652, with approximately 1,000 Preston fans.

I was still down at the steps leading to the upper part of the Kop as the game kicked off. I was just ready to go to my seat when a Preston player went down like a sack of spuds in the penalty area and the ref pointed to the spot with 43 seconds on the clock. I will have to see this again as it looked like a dive to me and I felt he'd conned the ref. Unfortunately Blackman was unable to save the penalty, going the wrong way, which for once I predicted correctly. An uphill battle beckoned. Straight away Preston started with time-wasting tactics and I said the ref wouldn't book anyone until the last few minutes and I was right about that. A terrible referee who let Preston walk all over him, especially by letting the time wasting go unpunished. With new players in the team, it took a while for them to start playing football, but once we did their keeper saved a great shot on target from Shackleton. With 30 minutes gone, Preston were reduced to ten men after their player was sent off, which he deserved, for a two-footed tackle on Baker. We had a great chance to equalise but Jansson's header was cleared off the line. Bamford was unlucky not to score with two great chances, but their goalkeeper was leading a charmed life and made another fantastic save to deny him. One move was out of this world, which their goalie saved. Just before half-time, and despite all the Leeds pressure, their player beat off challenges to run from near the half-way line to score Preston's second goal. That was a vital goal for them and made it even harder for us.

At half-time, when I was talking to my friend Margaret, we both agreed that we thought we were playing Norwich again due to the kit Preston were wearing. Unfortunately the score at half-time was different to Saturday. I wasn't too downbeat at this time because we were attacking, had shots on target and had been unlucky not to get back into the game.

The second half saw a double substitution, with Klich on for Shaughnessy and Saiz for Shackleton. The subs made an instant impact as Saiz made some great runs, and once again Bamford came close to scoring. As the game went on, Roberts tried to do a flick with the ball which didn't work as he expected. I said straight away that he would be subbed and he was, more or less straight after this, with Alioski coming on to replace him. I didn't think he'd had a good game either. The longer the game went on, you just knew we weren't going to get anything out of it, which was impacted by the play acting and time wasting from Preston. That said, Preston didn't sit back and defend once they had their player sent off, and if a neutral fan was watching I think they'd have been pleased to see an end-to-end game. From a Leeds perspective though, it turned out to be our first defeat of the season. I also thought that Bamford looked very lightweight in attack near the end of the game. Whether his fitness wasn't up to scratch I don't know, but, watching him closely as Leeds were attacking the Kop end, I found out that I wasn't impressed with what I was seeing. Despite losing the game, there were plenty of positives to be had. Bielsa had kept Phillips in the spine of the team, and with the strongest bench I've seen Leeds have for a long time I felt he was taking the game seriously. We did lots of attacking with shots on target and had an opposition keeper playing out of his skin. Maybe if he'd have been booked early in the first half for all the time wasting he was doing, it may have impacted on his game. Pearce was limping for a lot of the second half with a muscle injury by the look of it. We'd no subs left but credit to him for carrying on and without making a fuss about it.

I know many Leeds fans aren't interested in the cup games anymore and feel the league is more important. That is something I don't agree with as winning breeds winning. I didn't feel the same way tonight as I did after the defeats against Sutton and Newport, because we had been trying and did put some great attacks in where we were unlucky not to score. Back at Elland Road on Friday for our game against Middlesbrough sees an important game for us in the top-of-the-table clash; I am happy that Peacock-Farrell will be back in goal. Whilst I have nothing against Blackman, he seemed to hesitate when getting the ball out from the back and I think that was picked up by Bielsa at the end of the game. For once I didn't feel too disappointed about the defeat and as we play Preston again in September at Elland Road that will be the game where the points matter.

MIDDLESBROUGH (H) – 31 AUGUST 2018

As my granddaughter Laura and I headed to Elland Road for the near sell out clash, I found I literally had to drag myself there. It was a real effort as I felt that bad, but I realised that work overload issues had affected me more than I'd have ever thought. With the Peacock buzzing and everyone in high spirits, I knew that my Leeds United family and team would come to the rescue. To the lad in the Peacock who hadn't found my Stoke photos, the link to them is here http://www.followmeandleedsunited.co.uk/stoke-city-5th-august-2018-at-elland-road, so hopefully you will find the photo you are looking for. With my daughter Dani as well, we headed into the ground early as we knew there would be queues. My friends Sue and Paul were still stuck in traffic at that point, so hopefully they made it for kick-off.

The team: Peacock-Farrell, Berardi, Ayling, Cooper, Klich, Alioski, Saiz, Roofe, Harrison, Phillips and Douglas. Subs: Jansson for Berardi (88), Bamford for Roofe (90) and Dallas for Harrison (90+2). The game ended in a 0-0 draw, which saw Leeds remain at the top of the league going into the international break. Attendance was 35,417, with 2,322 Boro fans.

Today was always going to be a tough one, this being a top-of-the-table clash, with Boro being in second place. I wasn't sure how this would go as all the talk was of Boro having some very tall players in their side. I liked what Bielsa had to say in his press conference though, he comes across very humble but is looking at what he has to do to try and win the game and it is very refreshing to hear him speak. I knew then that we may do something different at times tonight. As the game kicked off, I thought at times we looked a bit nervous and we started to play the long ball as well as our passing being a bit short. I thought we needed to play to our strengths and pass the ball between us, and once we settled down I thought we handled the game very well. We had another atrocious referee, who was booking our players left, right and centre, whereas a Boro player actually got booked for dissent rather than the foul. One foul on Harrison should have warranted a card but lo and behold that one was play on. With the whole ground in good voice, it lent to the atmosphere which was great to hear from a packed Elland Road. Peacock-Farrell made a great save from Jonny Howson and then we had Ayling's header kicked off the goal line. When Roofe went down in the penalty area the ref waved play on. At half-time I was told that both teams should have had a penalty, although I couldn't remember a specific incident for Boro.

The second half continued with end-to-end football. Boro were proving tough opposition, which wasn't unexpected, and I was hoping our fitness levels would get us there in the end. Peacock-Farrell made a great save to deny them and Harrison had a great shot that went just wide. I thought he played very well today as there had only been flashes of brilliance against Preston on Tuesday. Game time I'm sure is what he has been lacking. We started attacking a lot, and with one move Saiz had the ball and should have sent a first time ball out to Alioski on the wing next to him. Unfortunately, he kept hold of the ball for longer than he needed, and when he did pass it Alioski had strayed offside. I thought we were going to stick with the same team and not bring on any subs. When Berardi went down injured in the penalty area in front of the South Stand, the trainer didn't come on to the pitch and he carried on. He didn't last long after that and, as I saw him limping, Bielsa was already on it and Jansson was coming on to the pitch to replace him. With the last kick of the game, we won a free kick just outside the box but weren't able to put the ball into the net. What celebrations there would have been if it had gone in? As it was, we had to settle for a point but I was happy to take that. We remain unbeaten going into the international break and then we head to Millwall where last year they kicked our unbeaten run into touch.

After seeing that the Children's Heart Surgery Fund (CHSF) will be the club's Charity of the Year for the 2018/19 season, all I can say is this is a worthwhile charity and I look forward to seeing how Leeds United support them over the season. As my daughter Charlotte died from congenital heart disease at 17 days old, I know exactly what families go through and wouldn't wish the pain on anyone. If she'd have been sent to Leeds at the time, there was the chance she would have been able to live a normal life. Sadly she never got that.

CHAPTER 3

MILLWALL (A) – 15 SEPTEMBER 2018

When I got up at the unearthly hour of 5.20am, it could only be for one thing – a Leeds United away day, and, as it turned out, a 17-hour round trip. This was the first game after the international break so it was nice to see the football back. It was quite dark and drizzly as I left home to travel to Leeds and shows the nights are drawing in. After picking up at Wakefield and Chesterfield, we headed to Bexleyheath for a short pub stop. We actually got a good welcome and a very big thank you to the manager and staff for reserving tables for us, which were most unexpected. The manager's uncle is a Leeds fan and we got great feedback from him, saying we were the best football fans they'd ever had there. From there we headed to the police escort and thought we'd just missed one as there was a coach at the far side of the common with the police. We were made to park on the grass and as some fans on the coach were making their way off it, as we were to be kept there for a while, it was good to hear we were heading off after all. They took four of the coaches in as another three pulled up at our first stop on the common and stayed behind. We had an uneventful escort in, apart from the coach driver beeping the horn so many times due to the London drivers trying to encroach into the escort. The Millwall fans we did see were their usual selves with their gestures, which I'm sure would have been reciprocated by some of the Leeds

fans. We did get a salute from some lads walking further on so knew they were ours. The reception committee at the ground was quite large but didn't feel as intimidating as in the past. We heard that lots of Leeds fans were caught up in traffic due to Rotherhithe Tunnel being closed, which meant some didn't get to the ground until half-time.

A big thank you to Bob, Dean, Skippa, Olivia and Ella for buying my new book *Back to Reality, Leeds United 2017-18* and I'm grateful for the support. John has ordered all five of my books and I look forward to getting a photo of him in due course, plus Nikki, Stephen and Rita, who have bought all five books too. I was going to put my flag up at the back of the stand next to the New Wrexham Whites flag that Brian had brought. One of our stewards shouted that there was some netting at the far right of the seats so I went to put it there instead. As it was, by doing that I managed to meet up with all the people I had to see either before, at half-time or near the end of the game. Hooter's son Aleksy was going to run around the pitch at half-time so, as well as looking for Samuel Becchio doing his job on the pitch, I had more photos to get. I'd already promised to get photos of our mascot and managed to get some to share with his dad. Reuben, Dylan's son, also helped me to put my flag up, so thank you. As I nipped downstairs just before the kick-off I realised I'd forgotten to go and take some photos of a group of Garforth Whites but luckily was able to catch up with them.

With an injury list that was growing with the long-term absences of Hernandez, Bamford, Berardi and Roofe, it was going to be interesting to see how Bielsa managed this. As it was, there were only two changes, with Jansson and Roberts being the two brought in.

The team: Peacock-Farrell, Ayling, Cooper, Jansson, Douglas, Harrison, Saiz, Alioski, Phillips, Roberts and Klich. Subs: Baker for Klich (61), Dallas for Roberts (68) and Forshaw for Phillips (74). Attendance was 17,195, with 2,220 Leeds fans. The game ended in a 1-1 draw, with Harrison equalising for Leeds in the 89th minute.

After last year's capitulation here, which then impacted on the way we were going to play, it meant no one knew what to do; I felt we never recovered from that. We played a different game from then on, which led to the eventual sacking of Christiansen and the short termism of Heckingbottom. The good thing this year, which has given me more confidence, is the appointment of Bielsa as our manager. I like him immensely as he has got the team fitter and has them playing how I want to see it, with lots of attacking football. There will be ups and downs no doubt, but I wasn't coming here today expecting us to lose. I'd only got butterflies in my stomach on the last part of the journey on the coach, as on previous visits things have been thrown at the coaches. Luckily nothing like that happened today. As the game kicked off, though, I thought Jansson looked a little nervy along with a few of the others, but we managed to contain Millwall and started to get some good attacks of our own going. There were quite a few misplaced passes for a while too. After Alioski was caught offside again, many fans were saying he was always being caught offside. With one, though, I thought he ran from behind their players so couldn't understand why the flag went up. Unless I get to see that attack again, I won't know for sure. Roberts got in a good position a few times but there was not enough power to the chances unfortunately. Millwall had a few chances and Morison, after his recent mouthing off in the press about being Zlatan, was kept under wraps for a lot of the game before he was subbed. The height of Jansson was vital today, and whilst his passing at first was shaky, his headers were superb. The first half went very quickly so I stayed at the front of the stand to take the photos before going downstairs just before the second half kicked off. As I got there I immediately heard my name shouted as some of the Halifax Whites were there with Shuy, who was over from Australia. One of the lads had his son Jake with them, but he wasn't there for the photo. Shuy looks forward to reading my blog in Australia and a big thank you to the others for their comments. To be told that I do a fantastic job with my blog, to keep doing it and not to take any notice of any negativity is greatly appreciated.

The second half had just kicked off as I got back to my seat, and there were many fans standing in the aisles this time. I'm not sure if we were slow off the mark, but Millwall took the lead 11 minutes into it when we failed to clear the ball. That woke their fans up, who had been pretty poor, but it could have been because they knew we weren't going to be a walkover today. For a while we seemed to struggle, especially when Baker came on for Klich. He'd left his shooting boots at home as his shot landed at the front of the upper tier we were on. The one good thing about Bielsa is he doesn't dwell on making subs and if he needs to change things he will. When Roberts was subbed, Harrison ended up as striker which mystified a lot of fans. I commented with another that I expected Bielsa to know what he was doing. When the clock got to the 80th minute, I headed to the far side of the stand to get my flag, only stopping to talk to some fans first. As I got over to my flag I started to untie one side as Leeds had an attack and I stopped what I was doing, only to see Harrison get the ball and unleash a shot from the edge of the penalty area. As I watched to see where it went, the stand erupted with jubilant Leeds fans as the ball hit the back of the net to equalise in the 89th minute. Fantastic scenes of celebrations happened, but my heart was in my mouth as one lad balanced on the top of the wall on the stairwell with a large drop at the other side. I'd seen one of our players hurtling over to the other side then saw Bielsa getting involved as something kicked off in the Millwall area. As Saiz had a lot of fouls to skirt around, maybe something had been said to him. We got on with the game quickly though. It wasn't a case of settling for a draw, we were going to try for a winner. We did come close, before the final minutes saw us battle for our lives as Millwall tried to get a winner. Every Leeds player stood up to be counted and played their part in those closing minutes, which was good to see. We also broke out to attack and we looked as if we could finish the game strongly. As the whistle blew and the Leeds fans sang we were top of the league, I hadn't realised that Boro had lost but also, even before the game, I'd forgotten where we were in the table. Out of sight, out of mind means there is no hope for me. The Leeds fans were happy to stay in the stand for a while, celebrating as the Millwall fans were happy to stay and give abuse to us. This was reciprocated from our fans as gestures between both sets of fans carried on for ages.

Eventually, I got downstairs and heard the coaches were being kept in for a while, which wasn't unexpected. After taking photos of plenty of happy Leeds fans, we got back on the coach ready for our police escort away from the ground. With the police vans at the front and those on horseback to the left of us, it was quite funny seeing officers walking alongside the coaches to the right of us. Although we went out via Westminster Bridge again (there were plenty of tourists around despite the recent terrorist attacks), the journey didn't seem to take so long as last year as we got back to the M1. That was before we had the normal motorway queues when it went down to one lane and we got stuck in a load of traffic; normality resumes for us Leeds fans travelling back to Yorkshire as it wouldn't be an away day without it! I would have taken a draw at the start of the game and it was a hard-fought point which saw Leeds remain unbeaten (the only club in the Championship) and top of the league. Tuesday sees the first of two home games with the visit of Preston, who beat us in the Carabao Cup game a couple of weeks ago. This time it will be different I'm sure. We also have Birmingham at home on Saturday and I know we have lots of our overseas fans attending that one.

Before I finish today, my sincere condolences go to two of our long-term loyal Leeds fans who died on the same day last week. Fotis came from Salonika, Greece, and came twice a year to games and was always a guest of the Griffin branch of the Leeds United Supporters' Club. Mick Thompson, aka Trapper, was one of my lads from the Selby Branch that I ran in the 80s-90s. These deaths hit home and they will both be sadly missed. RIP lads and my thoughts are with all their families and friends.

PRESTON (H) – 18 SEPTEMBER 2018

Today saw the first of two home games in a week. With Preston having beaten us in the Carabao Cup, I said that we wouldn't make the same mistake again, but it wouldn't be easy. As I was meeting Vicky in the Peacock, who had bought my new book *Back to Reality, Leeds United 2017-18* for her dad as a birthday present, I wanted to get there early. I left my other half in the car whilst I headed there, and Terje from Norway shouted hello to me so I had to start with my photo taking. After a good chat with Ella and her dad, we went to queue for a drink but it was heaving at the bars. I couldn't believe that the extra beer huts in the Peacock garden were shut tonight as they'd been open for the cup game recently. I'd lost Ella by then, so stood talking to Karl and a lad from Halifax and stayed there as they waited to be served. The Peacock had missed a trick tonight as it took ages for the queues to go down. My daughter Dani and I headed into the ground as I wanted to be in place for the team coming out.

The team: Peacock-Farrell, Ayling, Cooper, Jansson, Harrison, Roberts, Alioski, Saiz, Klich, Douglas and Phillips. Subs: Dallas for Roberts (86), Forshaw for Klich (88) and Baker for Saiz (90). Leeds won the game 3-0, with goals from Cooper (37) and Roberts (74 and 82). Attendance was 27,729, with 306 Preston fans. (I knew there weren't many of them but that's a very poor turn out in comparison to the cup game. No doubt they'll cite it was cheaper for that one!)

The opening spell saw Preston taking the game to Leeds as they tried to build on their recent win, with Peacock-Farrell making a couple of saves early on. As long as they weren't handed any early penalties, I thought we would be okay. We had a couple of great chances then, which ended up with one kicked off the line, and although we had another great chance the finishing was poor. Jansson had stepped up a gear tonight and it looked like having played the whole game against Millwall had done him good. Although I thought he'd hesitated with his first pass up the field, he grew into the game and he got in on the act with some great footwork as the team fought and backed each other up. As Alioski went through on goal towards the South Stand, he was goalward bound when the linesman, in front of the West Stand, saw a lone player there and stuck his flag up late, just as Alioski sent a great ball into the bottom of the net. When fans keep complaining about him being offside, I think they need to take into account the amount of times the linesmen haven't got a clue. Alioski was running all over the pitch and some of the balls he got to he didn't have a right to get to them, one of them being when he raced over to the West Stand side and got the ball right on the line before playing a great pass to one of our players. We took the lead eight minutes before the break after the corner played in by Douglas was met by Cooper's diving header. Prior to the goal, Preston were once again time wasting and we had plenty of fouls not given our way which should have been. The linesman at the East Stand missed most things and it was unbelievable that he didn't see a bad shirt pull on Cooper that happened right in front of him. It looked like someone said something in his ear every time he ignored it! Once we'd scored the goal, though, the time

wasting disappeared for some reason. When Alioski chased after their player from the South Stand to the half-way line, he more or less got the ball, but as their player went down like a ton of bricks, the ref booked Alioski. I don't think it was a booking, though – yes, a foul for a free kick but he let so much more go from Preston. We were unlucky not to get a second goal to go into the break.

After finding Dean to hand over the books he and Skippa bought from me at Millwall, I headed back to my seat for the second half. We had an early chance when Jansson's header looked to be heading into the goal, only to be deflected wide. It looked like Preston came out with renewed vigour then, especially as they were more bothered about scoring now. They did in fact get the ball into the net for an equaliser, or so I thought, until the cheers from the Leeds fans when the linesman put his flag up for offside saw it disallowed, thank goodness. As the game continued I was surprised to see that Bielsa wasn't looking to make any changes to the team. He kept crouching down in different parts of the technical area. I said to Dani that it looked like he wanted to give those playing a run out, which then saw them all step up a gear. Some of the passing and movements were out of this world, and one of the attacks was outstanding. What we saw tonight was some absolutely fantastic football and it didn't end there. After Harrison (we saw how the run had helped him with some great footwork) hit the post after some immense work from Saiz, we got a second goal. Phillips put a perfect pass over for Roberts to run onto and lob the ball over the keeper. Some great celebrations followed then, and, despite what Millwall's manager said, they weren't reserved just for them! To cap it all we got a third, again after some great play from

Saiz, who played the ball out to Klich, whose pin-point pass saw a cool Roberts head the ball into the net. That was it, game over, and to see the football we have witnessed tonight was absolutely fantastic. The team went off to a standing ovation and it was well deserved. When my hubby said that it reminded him of Wilkinson tonight, I said no Bielsa reminds me of Don Revie. If he can emulate what he and the team achieved then we are in for some great times. I like Bielsa and what he and his coaching staff have done so far with the team. He doesn't slag anyone off, just gets on with it, and I look forward to Saturday when we meet Mr Monk and Birmingham.

BIRMINGHAM (H) – 22 SEPTEMBER 2018

With today's game a sell-out, it was good to see our worldwide fan base coming together. Although I missed our Hong Kong Whites who were outside the Peacock when my daughter Dani arrived, it was good to know that plenty of our Scandinavian fans and Irish fans would be here today. As my granddaughter Laura and I headed to the Peacock, where I was hoping to meet up with some of the Not606 Forum members, I remembered that I had to buy a programme today. On the Supporters' Club page were two photos of my granddaughter Hannah and me from our recent visit to Berlin, one taken in Stockport International airport and the other by the Brandenburg Gate with us both wearing our Leeds shirts with pride. After the recent atrocious weather, it was nice to stand in the garden and chat to plenty of Leeds fans. Speaking to one of our lads later, who is at the front of the Kop, he said he was soaked to the skin after the Preston game mid-week. Unfortunately, due to his wheelchair, he had to stay put and was the only one in his group who got saturated sadly. I found the people who I needed to and it was good to meet up and chat, before both of my sisters Karin and Erica arrived with a friend. It's not often we get a photo of all three of us at Elland Road at the same time, but thank you Laura for doing that for me. When Chris Turton came to say hello, he said the last time he'd seen me there was no thought of me having children or grandchildren, so that shows how long ago it was. It was good to meet him and his family.

I know I shouldn't get superstitious, but I tried to banish the thought of Birmingham not having won so far this season. I wish those stats were never mentioned because it always turns out wrong for us. In discussions before the game I said I wouldn't get carried away as there is a long way to go yet, and I would rather just keep getting the points and see what happens later in the season. With Monk coming back as their manager, too, I didn't want him to have the satisfaction of becoming the first team to beat us this season in the Championship, but sadly that became the case. It felt as if his ghost at Elland Road had a detrimental effect on our team's game today.

The team: Peacock-Farrell, Ayling, Cooper, Jansson, Harrison, Douglas, Phillips, Roberts, Saiz, Alioski and Klich (an unchanged team). Subs: Dallas for Phillips (34), Forshaw for Klich (62) and Edmondson for Douglas (71). Leeds lost the game 2-1, with Alioski getting the Leeds goal (85). Attendance was 34,800, with 1,314 Birmingham fans. Eight minutes of injury time was added on at the end of the second half, the majority for time wasting.

Before I go on, the ref today was an absolute disgrace to the profession. Conned time after time with play acting and time wasting, why did he wait until eight minutes from the end to book one of their players for the latter? You could see him getting a flea in his ear after stopping the game again in the second half. He could have put a stop to it in the first half instead of letting Birmingham dictate the game that way. As someone said after the game, they reckoned he wasn't fit enough to keep up with play and kept wanting a rest. That wouldn't have been so bad if he hadn't ignored the amount of fouls on Saiz and booked him when he complained about the time wasting. It is time that the EFL stood up to be counted with the number of referees we have already had this season who should be demoted because they are not good enough!

That said, we lost the game within the first 20 minutes as we failed to play to our strengths and let in two soft goals. It was one of those moments when you felt that playing three games within the last week had taken its toll on us. Our passing wasn't crisp enough and we were letting Birmingham get the better of us and didn't close them down enough. When their attack ended with Peacock-Farrell committed to the wrong side of the goal as the ball was struck into the right-hand side from where I was looking from the Kop, I was sure no one deflected it. I think that was the case as he was anticipating where the ball was going, rather than waiting to make the save. It was a soft goal to give away though. From there things didn't really improve for us either as we seemed to be playing more to the benefit of Birmingham rather than our strengths. Pumping balls into the air when they had massive players, who were able to bully us, seemed counterproductive. We were too slow to the ball quite a few times too. It was no surprise when they got a second goal as we had struggled to make an impact on the pitch. It was still another soft goal though as no one closed their player down as he hit the ball, which went in via the post. Phillips was subbed just after this, although no one collectively was really playing well at that moment. He had Douglas in space on the left-hand side of the pitch but ran across to the right instead and was caught in possession, but no one was helping him either. Peacock-Farrell made a great save to deny them a third goal prior to a good move from Leeds, when a great chance fell to Alioski but his shot was blasted over the bar.

The second half struggled to get going because, as always, when we have to play the officials as well, it never works out for us. The linesman missed a blatant shirt pulling in the penalty area too. With Birmingham players falling like flies and the ref blowing up all the time to slow the game down, it took us until the 85th minute to pull a goal back, when Alioski put the ball into the net in front of the Kop. There was a small celebration as he raced back to the half-way line for them to get on with the game. It's ironic how we didn't need the trainer on the pitch after being fouled though, as our players got on with it! When eight minutes of injury time was put up it gave us a chance to get an equaliser and we nearly did get that, when Dallas's shot was saved by their goalie to deny us a point. We did battle in the latter parts of the game to get back into it, but it was probably too little too late.

After the game I headed to Green Hammerton with my other half for a charity evening to hear Ian playing from vinyl, his Motown and Soul music. Ian said I was at the beach playing football with his friend in Salonika in 1973 as we were on the same trip; it's a small world really! On our way home, we encountered animals on the road as we ground to a halt just before the junction of the A58. All I could think of was the Leeds vile animals for some reason, oops.

Despite losing for the first time this season (apart from the Carabao Cup), we have to pick ourselves us and get on with it. The defeat was always going to happen at some point sadly, and for those calling for Peacock-Farrell to be dropped, the answer to that from me is no! We have to build our team around him and have to take the ups and downs that will happen along the way. I know fans are entitled to their opinion, but this team is being built for the future as well so we march on to our next game on Friday to Sheffield. I will be driving to this one with my daughter Dani straight from work.

SHEFFIELD WEDNESDAY (A) – 28 SEPTEMBER 2018

As soon as I finished work, I got quickly changed into my Leeds things and headed over the tops to Wakefield from Brighouse as I was driving to the game today. After making good time I picked up my daughter at Junction 39, and although there was some traffic as we pulled off the M1, we got

to the ground early enough to get a good parking spot at the garage. As I pulled into the forecourt I was going to go out again and pull in at the side of the pumps, but thanks to Paul I stayed where I was and we parked for free.

Because we arrived so early the turnstiles weren't even open so we headed to the players' entrance just in time for the team to arrive. Before they got there, though, we were asked if we could be filmed for Sky TV. As we said yes, they wanted us to do a fist pump so we both automatically did the Leeds salute! We were tagged in a photo of it later (this had been played at the start of the game), and it was really good quality.

The first thing we did was head to the front of the stand to hang my flag up and I was allowed to put it on the stairs going down to the lower tier. It wasn't a surprise to find out a few of the stewards were Leeds United fans though, and thanks to all of them who helped me and let me take a photo of my flag. I had a chat to a Spurs fan steward and only moved at the start of the game, heading to my seat. I'd like to say a big thank you to Dawn and Paul for buying my new book *Back to Reality, Leeds United 2017-18* for their little granddaughter, who attended her first game last week. As always I appreciate the support.

The team: Peacock-Farrell, Ayling, Cooper, Douglas, Harrison, Jansson, Saiz, Alioski, Roberts, Klich and Phillips. Subs: Forshaw for Saiz (90). The game ended in a 1-1 draw, with Klich getting the Leeds goal with a spectacular strike (62). Attendance was 26,717, with 4,600 Leeds fans.

I'm glad I'm on the same wavelength as Bielsa as I'm adamant we have to stick with what we are trying to do. There will be ups and downs but he stuck with the same team again, making no changes. After last year's defeat here and with us losing our first league game, I thought we wouldn't be making the same mistake as against Birmingham last week. That said it didn't stop my stomach churning half-way through the first half though.

The game saw the first half pass really quick with a lot of end-to-end stuff. Although some of our passing wasn't crisp enough there were a few nervous minutes before we settled down. Some Wednesday players tried to emulate the Birmingham players by being 'injured' on the floor. One of the moves we did though, when five of our players were like flies around one of their players and won the ball cleanly, had us shaking our heads with astonishment. For the life of me I couldn't understand why the free kick was given against us, especially as just before that Saiz had been fouled and it was play on. He was playing some fantastic stuff once again and won us a corner. We came very close to taking the lead then, with Douglas hitting the post and Phillips having to settle for the rebound being cleared off the line. We started to play really well at that point as we put pressure on the Wednesday goal. We weren't having it all our own way though and Peacock-Farrell was called on to make a good save to deny them a goal. Despite what a few fans around me said, he didn't stand a chance with the goal they scored just before half-time. When the ball was launched into the air it looked like it was sailing over the goal, only to hit the post and go into the net. That was a real downer at the time as it came out of the blue, but Cooper brought a save out of their keeper just before the break. Put it this way, I bet if he tried to do that again he would never score in a month of Sundays!

The second half saw me asking the lad next to me whether the photographers in front of the stand to the right of the goal knew something we didn't? There were a number of them who had positioned themselves in front of the Leeds fans, obviously waiting for us to score. We didn't disappoint them either when Klich went on to equalise with a spectacular goal. Although they had a couple of chances, at times we were camped in their half. What I really liked seeing was Leeds not letting the ball go out for a throw in but keeping the ball in play, along with carrying on the attack. What we saw on the pitch at times in that second half was some absolutely brilliant stuff, which was fantastic to see. Despite all the pressure, though, we couldn't get a winning goal even though we came close. At times we were like a battering ram and some of the moves were out of this world. I wasn't too disappointed at the end of the game, even though some were saying that we had dropped two points. We may have battered them and only had one goal to shout about, but at one time we would have lost that game so I am happy we got a point and weren't beaten. The progress we are making on the pitch even with the long-term injuries we have bodes really well for the future. With another week ahead where we have three games to contend with, I wonder what will happen this time. One of these days, we will get the rub of the green when we play like we did tonight.

CHAPTER 4

HULL CITY (A) – 2 OCTOBER 2018

This was the second time in a week that I was heading to an away game straight from work, only this time the Fullerton Park coach was taking the strain. I arrived at Elland Road at the same time as my daughter Danielle and had a chat to Fiona Hanley, the Supporters' Liaison Officer (SLO) for Leeds, before getting on the coach. We seemed to arrive in Hull in no time at all and found out why there was to be no parking around the ground, due to the big Hull Fair situated on the car parks. As we were escorted through the site, I couldn't help but notice the great amount of impressive mobile homes there were. Obviously they must be doing okay!

Once in the ground I headed to the front to hang my flag up, although I was disappointed when I went back to get it near the end of the game and found it had been knocked to the floor. What a shame no one tied it back up again. I also couldn't believe that we had only been given 2,100 tickets for this game either. When they had such a small attendance with no end of empty seats, it doesn't make sense that they would turn down extra money that we would generate by selling us more, as once again we sold out our allocation in minutes; they must have more money than sense. The one thing they did have right though was having loads of beer being served at once, something that has been mentioned to Angus Kinnear recently that needs improvement at Leeds. The one thing that was over the top in my opinion was the number of police in attendance dressed in riot gear.

The team: Peacock-Farrell, Ayling, Cooper, Jansson, Phillips, Klich, Harrison, Douglas, Alioski, Saiz and Roberts. Subs: Forshaw for Saiz (74), Dallas for Harrison (74) and Shackleton for Douglas (82, went off injured). Leeds won the game 1-0 with a goal from Roberts (51). Attendance was 13,798, with 2,100 Leeds fans.

As the game kicked off, Leeds started with plenty of possession and on the attack, coming close in the opening minutes. At that time I thought some of the Hull players looked scared as I wanted us to take charge of the game. At times our build up was slow and we had some sloppy passing. At other times we were passing the ball between ourselves and wearing Hull down. We should have taken the lead with Alioski through on goal but his final shot was wide. I thought the ball had taken a deflection or hit the post first, but I may be wrong with that. We should have also taken the lead just before half-time when Alioski's cross came to Douglas, who seemed to have an open goal in front of him; unfortunately, he blasted the ball over the top of the goal. That was an excellent chance and showed again that we can create chances but need to take them.

Thank you to Whitby John for buying my new book *Back to Reality, Leeds United 2017-18*. It was nice to hear that Olivia, who bought the same book at Millwall, has taken it to school to read. As she is the only Leeds fan surrounded by Bradford fans, she is doing an excellent job of flying the flag for us!

At the start of the second half it didn't take long before we took the lead with an excellent goal from Roberts. He let fly from outside the box and the ball beat their keeper, which was unexpected according to some of the fans near me. I hoped that would settle the nerves a bit. We had shouts for a penalty turned down, surprise, surprise, when the ball hit their player's hand(s) in the area, plus when Saiz fell in the area he was booked for diving. We saw plenty of the ball, but to me it looked like we were playing a slower game today. With us having three games again this week, I felt that impacted on the way we played tonight and we were preserving our energy. It wasn't one of the better games to watch from the terraces, but at the end of the day we got three points and the win which took us back to the top of the table. Leeds were fighting for the ball as Hull started to put some pressure on us. I just didn't want them to get anything out of the game at all, but we managed to keep them out thankfully.

At the end of the game the team had come over to the Leeds fans to clap us when all of a sudden Cooper came up holding a Leeds shirt with the words 'STAY STRONG TOBY' on it. That gesture brought tears to my eyes as we learnt yesterday that despite Toby overcoming his treatment for Neuroblastoma, he has now got a brain tumour. Keep fighting little man and I really hope you can overcome this too.

After arranging to meet someone in the Peacock for my book on Saturday at 1.45 pm, I'd checked on my calendar as I suddenly had the feeling the kick-off time had changed. I thought the Leeds fixtures would change automatically but they didn't, so I've rearranged my arrival time now.

I also had a French Journalist for *FRANCE FOOTBALL*, the main football magazine in France, contact me. The football magazine is the one that rewards 'The best player of the year' with The Ballon d'Or (The Golden Ball). Hopefully, I will meet up with him at the Brentford game as he said he would be interested to meet a true Leeds fan and a well-known blogger! It is nice to know that my blogs are being seen around the world.

BRENTFORD (H) – 6 OCTOBER 2018

As my granddaughter Hannah and I headed into Elland Road for the early kick-off after leaving at 8.30am, I realised that, despite feeling tired, many of our long-distance fans would have already been on the road a long time before. I was due to meet Christophe, the French journalist, for an interview in the Peacock at 10am but I hadn't expected it to still be shut when we got there. As Bev and Steve from Bournemouth were in Billy's bar and wanting my new book, I had to leave Hannah outside the door for five minutes in order to meet them. After bumping into Steve, who said that he remembered me from the 70s, we headed back across the road just in time to meet Christophe. We headed into the bottom part of the garden to do the interview as it would have been too noisy at the top with the band playing. I'm looking forward to the finished article, which he said would be sent to me, and I am grateful for the opportunity. Thank you also to the ladies on the table behind us who said that they had brought Frank with them, who had come to the game from Australia and was celebrating his birthday the next day. I hope he enjoys his day and the game. A few fans stopped for a photo during the interview and I got my flag out at the end for more photos. Bev and Steve, Pete and Lily, Karl and Louie, Garry for Aiden and Dylan, Peter, Craig and Michelle are all the proud owners of my new book and my grateful thanks go to them all for the support. Also, thanks to everyone who I spoke to who follows my blog and asked for photos, which is greatly appreciated. I was also given a LUSCOS badge from one of our Norwegian fans, which was a lovely gesture too. Annette and her niece from Denmark were also here for a regular visit to Elland Road.

Once in the ground, having met up with my daughter Danielle, she found her season ticket ended up having a lucky escape as she dropped it and it nearly went down the loo! I don't think things are that bad anymore lol! As we got to the top of the steps, a ball kicked from the pitch was heading straight above us until someone hit it and it bounced down just missing us and I nearly fell backwards trying to avoid it. Was someone trying to tell us something? I left most of my things in my seat as I headed to the front. I knew Dean was bringing his little girl to the game and I wanted to capture the occasion. Bless her she was so excited and had wanted to know why her picture wasn't in my new book? This means that I have to keep on doing these blogs and books because they tell the stories of Leeds fans following their team home and away. There were another couple of fans with Dean who had travelled from Australia for the game too. I then went to find Raymond, who was being filmed for the programme *The Undateables* again, as I wanted to get a photo. He was always found banging a tambourine at games over the many years he has followed Leeds.

The team: Peacock-Farrell, Ayling, Cooper, Jansson, Dallas, Saiz, Alioski, Klich, Roberts, Phillips and Harrison. Subs: Forshaw for Klich (63), Jack Clarke (one of our youngsters making his debut) for Dallas (70) and Baker for Saiz (76). Attendance was 31,880, with 510 Brentford fans. The score was 1-1, with Jansson equalising for Leeds (88).

Once again, for the umpteenth time this season, we had a 'referee' trying to make a name for himself when we were being shown live on Sky. How he can be called a professional with the way he conducted himself on the pitch is frankly unbelievable. It is about time that referees who cannot even get the basics right were accountable for their actions and demoted. It isn't a case of sour grapes or a referee not giving the home crowd many decisions. When Alioski slipped and lost the ball, with their man about a yard away, the ref blew for a foul in our favour! That was when I knew for sure he had lost the plot as everyone burst out laughing that the incredulous decision was given in the first place. All I want is a fair playing field, being allowed to challenge for a ball, win it without their player ending up on the floor and a free kick given even though we have come away with the ball. Football is a contact sport, but not receiving a head-butt from behind, as happened with Alioski later on in the game. He went to retrieve the ball from the Brentford dug-out to get on with the game, only for their coaches to play silly beggars, try and keep it and their player was totally out of order. When I think of the number of times we have had players hauled over the coals after the games had finished by the powers that be, I genuinely cannot understand why players are allowed to get away with it against us? There were still a fair few of their players going down 'injured' and time wasting, but not at the same level as a few teams have done recently.

With Douglas out injured after Hull City, it meant there would be a change to the team, and Dallas came in to replace him at left-back. I wasn't particularly enamoured with him playing so far back, but once again I put my trust in Bielsa to make the right decision. The fact that he wants players to be able to swap and change all over the pitch doesn't give me the same feeling of dread that we had under previous managers, when it was square pegs in round holes situations. As Brentford set off on the attack and Peacock-Farrell had to make a great save from them, we were going to have to keep on our toes today. That said, until the referee started blowing the whistle over any challenge that saw their player end up on the floor, I knew we were going to be up against 12 men again. With every challenge being given Brentford's way, when we did eventually get a free kick the referee was met with loud cheering from the crowd. Brentford had most of the chances in the first half, with Peacock-Farrell being called on to make numerous saves to deny them a goal. As our players had to run back and defend in numbers after being caught out of position when we attacked, it was good to see everyone working together in packs to win the ball back. We had a great chance to get a goal just before half-time, but Saiz's shot went wide after some great play between Alioski and Harrison.

The second half saw us trying to get a goal and we were unlucky not to score after their keeper fumbled the first shot but managed to stop Phillips get the rebound into the net. After a Brentford attack towards the South Stand, it looked like their chance had gone as the ball went past the post. With the fans going mad behind the goal, I realised he had given them a penalty! I haven't seen the action again but everyone said that their player was already falling before it got near Peacock-Farrell, but the ref decided he'd fouled him. Ten minutes after this incident it came up on Danielle's watch that Ayling had been booked for dissent! Unfortunately for us, Brentford scored the penalty, sending our keeper the wrong way, which sadly meant we had to come from behind again. When young Jack Clarke was brought on to make his debut, I said that maybe Ayling should come off as his passing had been quite poor today. I was wishing later on in the game that he had come off as the ref sent him off for a second bookable offence after a foul in the last minutes of the game. It was definitely a free kick, but when some of their players got away with fouls, why was Ayling not just given a talking to as it wasn't malicious just bad timing? As it was, Dallas came off, so I said Ayling may play better now, which he did until his sending off. Clarke had an immediate impact with a great cross into the box. We started to put the pressure on and I was particularly impressed today with both Alioski and Jansson. Alioski played at left-back at times once Dallas had come off, but the chasing down of balls, challenges and putting some great crosses in often bypass some of our fans. As the referee was getting lambasted by the Leeds crowd, this heightened the noise levels and upped the atmosphere. After winning a free kick two minutes from time, the Elland Road crowd went wild when, from it, Jansson headed home to equalise. As the players celebrated with the fans a few went on to the pitch, which resulted in one lad getting taken out. We were very unlucky not to win the game when it looked like Baker's header after Alioski had crossed the ball was going straight into the net. Unfortunately, it crept wide at the wrong side of the post so the game ended in a draw. It's a long time since I've heard chanting against the referee all around the ground. We've had plenty of poor ones over recent years, but this one today got up everybody's backs for his inept performance!

It was good to meet up with our Johannesburg Whites from South Africa after the game, although two have moved back to Yorkshire now to enable them to attend Elland Road more. It was nice to meet up with our West Coast Whites too, who are friends with one of our old Halifax lads, Daisy. When it was pointed out to me that they had three Bremner stones in the vicinity of mine I couldn't believe it!

With the international break upon us once again, the next game will be on 20 October, with another early kick-off for our visit to Blackburn. With a massive following of 7,650 Leeds supporters, my granddaughter Hannah is also coming to experience the away game with us. The last time she was at an away game was when we played Huddersfield the other year, but she was sat in the opposite end to us Leeds fans. With two of my daughters, Michelle and Danielle, and my granddaughter Laura, they had to keep their mouths shut when Leeds scored. At the end of the game, though, Hannah forgot where she was and cheered that Leeds had won, oops! Let's hope we can get the win at Blackburn!

BLACKBURN (A) – 20 OCTOBER 2018

It was still dark as we left home this morning for the noon kick-off and another live game for Sky. I was meeting my daughter Danielle in Leeds and was taking my granddaughter Hannah to her first away game with me. She was really excited and looking forward to her day out with over 7,600 Leeds fans. As there were no trains, Fullerton Park had two coaches going today and many other supporters were travelling by coach too. With our stop at our regular haunt of Leyland, they certainly had plenty of trade today, with fans standing at least four deep at the bar. Because of that I used the app for our food, which took the stress out of queuing.

We arrived at the services for our escort just as there was a convoy of coaches already being taken down to the ground. I was pleased to see that the police weren't messing about as we headed after them about five minutes later, going past all the queuing traffic on the opposite side of the road. There were loads of Leeds fans doing the salute to the coaches as we passed by with hardly any Blackburn fans in sight. As we were escorted past the ground, we began to wonder where we were being taken, but we were turning around at the end of the road, coming back and parking on the street. It was too late to go into the fan zone but it was good to see that being put in place for our fans once again. As Danielle and Hannah headed to the upper stand I went into the bottom stand, straight to the front, to put my flag up.

The team: Peacock-Farrell, Berardi and Roofe (both back from injury), Jansson, Cooper, Phillips, Klich, Alioski, Saiz, Roberts and Dallas. Subs: Hernandez for Roofe (70), Clarke for Dallas (76) and Shackleton for Berardi (86). Leeds lost the game 2-1, with Klich getting our goal right at the end of injury time in the first half (45+1). Attendance was 20,029, with 7,717 Leeds fans. Well done to Ella from our branch; she normally travels on our coach and was our mascot for the game.

As Leeds kicked off we went straight on the attack, but the final ball was mishit straight to their player. With their first attack they came straight to the goal in front of us, ending with two corners one after the other. We were left with an uphill battle once again when from the second one their player bullied us to head the ball straight into the top left-hand side of the goal right in front of us. My first thoughts were why didn't we have anyone defending on both sides of the goal as Bremner and Reaney used to do? It may be that they couldn't have done anything about the first goal, but when they scored a similar goal for their second it would have made a difference I'm sure, especially as that turned out to be the winner.

Saiz brought a save out of their keeper and we had to thank Peacock-Farrell a couple of times for stopping them taking a further lead. With the Leeds support getting behind the team, we were frustrated to see passes going astray, and when we did win corners Alioski's first few crosses were below par. In fact, it looked like the players were disjointed and Bielsa hadn't got the line up right from the start for this game. I'd said before the game that I hadn't seen us have square pegs

in round holes this season as everyone gets to play all over the pitch, so it hadn't been apparent. I think I should have kept my mouth shut, especially with Dallas at right-back, although he swapped sides with Berardi later on. We have a great young player in Pearce who can play at left-back in his rightful position and I would much rather play him than put Dallas in either position where he hasn't impressed me. There was a lot of frustration from the Leeds fans when we kept playing the ball out from the back but going from side to side until we could work our way forwards. As someone commented on the fact that we had been found out, I said we had to work out a different way to overcome them. We got one minute of injury time as we played out from the back; I said it would take us the full minute to get to the far end of the pitch. As we got to the far end after 13 passes in 45 seconds, the ball was in the net to equalise. What a relief to get the goal just before the whistle blew. We all agreed we had played to our strengths along the floor because any high balls were being mopped up by their set of giants in both attack and defence. I wondered what was in the water over here as well as what they were feeding them!

I went downstairs to hear some lads say we didn't deserve it; I said the team was being patient in their build ups, whereas the patience amongst many fans had worn thin, but we all agreed we would take the fact we had equalised. As the lad next to me in the seats said, how many times have we not deserved to have penalties, free kicks etc. given against us? We need things to even themselves out and go our way instead.

The second half saw Leeds straight on the attack and it looked like we would take the game by the scruff of the neck. At times we did do that but we weren't consistent enough. A couple of times we waited for the ball to go out rather than get it, only for Blackburn to nip in and take the ball off our toes. As we waited for Hernandez to come on as sub, I wondered why he hadn't come on before realising it was because Blackburn had got a free kick. Unfortunately, they got a corner out of it which resulted in Blackburn scoring their second goal of the game. I was cross that we hadn't learnt our lesson from the first half and put players on both posts as we could have avoided that one and kicked the ball off the line. When Roofe was battling in the left-hand corner near us to keep the ball from going out for a goal kick, he was holding his own until there were two of them attacking him. No one could believe it when the linesman put his flag up to give the free kick against us. As the conspiracy theories against us grow, we all feel that the officials don't even hide it now with their outrageous decisions that are so blatantly against us. Saiz brought out a great save from their goalie before we had two penalty shouts, one for a foul and one for hand ball. I would need to see them again, but after my neighbour said on my return home he'd heard them say on the TV that we had been robbed there must have been something in the non-decisions.

Unfortunately we couldn't manage an equaliser, despite the pressure put on by our players in the last minutes of the game. As the final whistle blew and we had our second defeat of the season, the dreaded curse of after the international break, a large away support from us, plus the early kick-off, have once again raised their head, sadly.

Thanks for my chocolates and Galway Whites badge Paul. After doing an away fan review for Dirk Copland of Blackburn Roverseas prior to the game, I did a follow-up one afterwards as requested too.

Thanks to Helen for buying my new book. Talking about my books, I just wanted to remind those fans who are thinking of Christmas presents that autographed copies are available from me. Just let me know where and when to meet and I'll sort it out. There are some great stories of life as a Leeds United fan ranging from the 70s until now, which cemented our loyal support for our team and is why we have the support we have today.

We move on to Wednesday's game against Ipswich at home when we have to pick ourselves up and get something out of the game. Having not picked up many points of late, we do need to turn things around – and soon. There were always going to be ups and downs and I feel that having the right team on the pitch at the start of the game is very important.

IPSWICH (H) – 24 OCTOBER 2018

We were later than usual getting to Elland Road for this night game as there seemed to be loads of traffic everywhere. On hearing the M621 was closed in both directions, we came off at Tingley instead and got there 40 minutes before kick-off. By the time we'd walked to the ground it was too late to go to the Peacock, although it meant I missed Paul, one of my Selby Whites, and Simon too, who will be heading back to Canada shortly. I missed my sister Erica but managed to see her in the North East lower when I got into the Kop so was able to have a chat as well as at Billy's statue

after the game. She made me laugh as the last few games she has attended she has gone in the North West, the East upper, North East lower and on Saturday she will be in the West Stand. As she said, though, it depended where the available tickets were! With the majority of our mid-week games being on a Tuesday, I had to be reminded that today was Wednesday too. Also, with having had a very stressful day at work, I was looking forward to the football taking my mind off things. Thank you to the gentleman who said he had enjoyed reading my book; *Once a Leeds fan, always a Leeds fan*, and I am grateful for the feedback.

The team: Peacock-Farrell, Cooper, Ayling (back from his one game suspension), Phillips, Berardi, Alioski, Saiz, Klich, Roofe, Hernandez and Harrison. Subs: Dallas for Berardi (went off injured) (27), Forshaw for Saiz (57) and Pearce for Harrison (57). Leeds won 2-0, with goals from Roofe (22) and Cooper (66). Attendance was 29,082, with approximately 500 Ipswich fans.

Having done an interview for Amy Downes and her blog *Diary of a Tractor Girl*, I said I'd no idea where any team was in the league as I only concentrate on Leeds United. Lo and behold, what did I keep hearing afterwards? Only that Ipswich were bottom of the table, which usually meant teams would play out of their skins against us. It better not be a banana skin tonight!

After hearing that Jansson got a one-game ban after his recent comments at the end of the Brentford game, I was fizzing. If I had my way, the ref from that game would never have got the chance again due to his absolute incompetence. When Jansson said the word s**t in his post-match interview, which in my view is quite tame in comparison to many swear words these days, then said we were robbed, he was only speaking the truth. As usual, there is one rule for Leeds United and one rule for everyone else! It's getting to feel like it is us against everyone else again, as per the -15 season, so if it has to be a siege mentality, then so be it.

As Leeds attacked the South Stand, we came close a couple of times. With their keeper out of position, Hernandez's shot from a long way out was off target. Alioski playing left-back put some hard crosses in, with one being saved by their keeper and the rebound just missing Hernandez. Alioski put in quite a few crosses, although they were too long but had plenty of power in them. He made some great runs down the left and I thought he played really well. Berardi got booked for a foul and was lucky to escape a talking to for another foul. I said I wanted to see 90 minutes of blood on their boots and then realised we had already played 20 minutes of the game. I didn't want to see Berardi get his marching orders though, which was always going to be a worry once he got an early booking. I couldn't tell that Ipswich were bottom of the table, though, as I thought they at least tried to play football and there was none of the cheating that had gone on previously with other teams. Just after Ipswich had a header saved by Peacock-Farrell, Leeds took the lead. Saiz battled to win the ball in the centre of the park, passed it out to Hernandez on the right wing, whose pass gave Roofe a delightful header that flew into the net. What a relief! That seemed to be the first time we had taken a lead for a while, but I could be wrong of course. A few minutes later Berardi went off injured and we had to reshuffle our formation. After the initial euphoria things quietened down on the terraces as the half-time whistle blew.

I came back up into the stand to hear the second half had already kicked off (you used to be able to see on the TVs when the team came back out but not anymore). As I got to the top of the steps the Kop shouted hand ball in unison. As I got back to my seat, Danielle my daughter said that it was definitely hand ball and right in front of the ref. It wouldn't have been a penalty though as it was outside the area. As Ipswich attacked the far end, I heard someone say they better not score now! As we started attacking more and more, their keeper ended up being their man of the match for me as he made some fantastic saves to deny us a further goal. Hernandez was playing really well and the team gained confidence as we continued to get behind their defence. We scored a second goal from a corner when the ball was passed across the box and Cooper hit it into the net. We nearly got a third, which looked destined for the top corner when Alioski unleashed a fantastic shot, only to see it bounce back out after hitting the top corner of the goalpost. We continued to put Ipswich under pressure and played some really good passing football, but on their rare attacks I was always wary they could pull a goal back. At least it was nice to see they didn't time waste their way through the game, which was a breath of fresh air after recent games. Leeds made a double substitution, with both Forshaw then Pearce coming on. I said that Harrison would go off and Alioski would move forward, with Pearce dropping back. Well of course that is what happened, so Bielsa and I are on the same wavelength lol.

The win put us back on top of the league and it was good to hear that West Brom had been battered by Derby. Saturday sees us back at Elland Road for the second home game in a few days but for a later kick-off of 5.30pm due to the match being televised live on Sky once again. Hopefully the win will have taken some of the pressure off the team and we can go out and enjoy ourselves, getting another three points.

NOTTINGHAM FOREST (H) – 27 OCTOBER 2018

Before I start my blog today, I wish to pay my respects to our oldest and longest Leeds United fan, Edna Newton, who died this week aged 94 years. Having a season ticket for 64 years was a fantastic achievement and the game needs more fans like her. It was a proud moment seeing my photo on the scoreboard on the 64th minute signalling the whole ground to start giving their applause to celebrate her lifelong support of Leeds United. RIP Edna. The WACCOE message board I frequent had organised some flowers for Edna to be placed at Billy's statue, which was a lovely gesture. Also, Leeds United put flowers on her seat with a Leeds scarf around them, which is another heartwarming gesture.

It is also the nearest home game to Armistice Day and the 100-year anniversary of the Battle of the Somme. So many died in the wars and seeing the horrendous conditions in the trenches in the First World War brings a lump to my throat. The poignant *Last Post* played by the bugler always gets to me. To all those soldiers who gave their tomorrows so we could have our today, I salute you.

With a slightly later set-off time than normal, I thought it would be a good idea to go to the White Rose en route to Elland Road, with Danielle my daughter and granddaughter Laura. With queues of traffic everywhere, we were lucky to get a parking spot despite there only being a few vacant. I never expected it to be like that so I'll avoid daytime shopping if I can in the future as I hate it being crowded. Give me a football crowd any day!

I actually prefer 5.30pm kick-offs to the lunchtime ones and on arrival at the packed Peacock everyone was in good spirits. With fans having longer before the game, it contributed to the atmosphere and I tried capturing a new song that some lads were trying to get going by video. It was good to catch up with friends, although only for a short while before we headed in to the ground. Having looked for the Leeds United Supporters' Trust collecting food for Leeds south and east foodbank, I found them on the way in so well done to them.

The team: Peacock-Farrell, Ayling, Dallas, Cooper, Jansson, Hernandez, Alioski, Klich, Phillips, Roofe and Forshaw. Subs: Pearce for Ayling (went off injured) (25), with Clarke replacing Pearce (65) and Saiz for Phillips (65). The game ended in a 1-1 draw, with Roofe equalising in the 84th minute. Attendance was 34,308, with 1,766 Forest fans.

After taking photos at the bottom of the steps, I made my way to my seat to find out that I nearly didn't have one! A man and woman had been sat in our season ticket seats when the other two got there. When Danielle had said they were in our seats they weren't for moving but one eventually did. They'd been overheard saying that if anyone asked them to move they'd be told to f**k off. I'm pleased to say that my seat had been vacated by the time I got there!

It took me ten minutes to realise that Dallas was playing at left-back again, which I wasn't exactly enamoured about. It made me think back to the Guiseley pre-season game when Dallas scored two goals from the left-hand side. Maybe that's behind Bielsa's thinking but whilst I've no problem him going forward I don't like seeing him in defence. It was just after this realisation that Forest took the lead from a corner, which meant we faced an upward battle again to get back on level terms. The Leeds crowd didn't let being a goal down deter them from keeping a good atmosphere going though. Ayling went down after being fouled, and although he got up again he only lasted a few minutes before being subbed. Looks like another big injury sadly, but I hope it isn't a repeat of last year's game against Forest which ended his season. Once they'd taken the lead, Forest started the time-wasting tactics, and when their man went down in the penalty area I thought he was feigning an injury. As he headed to the dugout rather than straight out to the touchline, I was just going to berate him but realised he was being subbed! Although we had a couple of chances, we didn't really test the Forest keeper, which was a contrast to the Ipswich game, with the amount of saves their goalie had to make.

The second half saw Forest still leading as Leeds ramped up the pressure. With the fans becoming the 12th man and getting behind the team, with WACCOE reverberating around the ground, we waited for a double substitution to be made when my photo of Edna came on the scoreboard. The applause for her was unanimous and I'm sure she'd have loved hearing the applause she received. I was surprised to see Pearce, himself a sub, taken off but realised Bielsa had pushed Alioski back and brought Jack Clarke on. He had an immediate impact when he put a low, hard cross across the box, which was crying out for someone to knock it in at the far post. We had an immense amount of pressure as Leeds tried their hardest to get an equaliser. A number of times the ball didn't fall kindly for us and I always felt like Forest would be a threat. I felt that as long as we kept them out and didn't give them a second we could get a goal and go on to win the game. The equaliser came in the 84th minute, with Saiz, Dallas and Klich involved before Roofe put the ball into the net to send the volume of eruption from the Leeds fans into overdrive. As we were heading back to the centre circle, I saw their keeper remonstrating with the linesman and claiming handball. As the referee headed over to the linesman, we waited with bated breath until he signalled to the centre spot. That was a relief, but I just thought it would have been carnage if they'd have disallowed it! Replays have apparently shown it was a ball to hand, but it's about time we had the rub of the green and the decision going our way for once. We had to settle for a point in the end but am happy to take that as it is better than a defeat. The one thing that we must do better is from our corners; we have to start beating the first man, which for some reason we cannot do more often than not. I don't like short corners but I could see why we resorted to them at times!

Thank you to Debbie and James for buying my new book *Back to Reality, Leeds United 2017-18*. With many fans saying they hadn't appeared in my photos as yet, including the original Donny

64 Consecutive seas
Marching on forever
Waccoe.com

Whites, that was remedied today! The latter may shout at me though as I wobbled so they'll have to ask me again next time they see me. As usual, many of our Scandinavian friends were in attendance, plus our Irish fans and we had some Utrecht fans visiting too. With plenty of others in attendance, including our long-distance South Coast regulars, it was nice to meet up with others after the game. Having just read that Rita, our Leeds United guide dog, and Nikki had an altercation with a Forest fan taking his anger out on them, all I can say is shame on you. How dare you attack them because that is nothing more than disgusting! On hearing there has been a helicopter crash at the King Power Stadium, Leicester, after their game, things aren't looking good after it burst into flames on impact. Sad times for their club.

We have a good break now, with our next game being against Wigan for the Sunday lunchtime kick-off. With another large following heading there, with tickets once again sold out in minutes, I hope we can do better than we did at Blackburn.

CHAPTER 5

WIGAN (A) – 4 NOVEMBER 2018

It seemed such a long time since we'd had a game at this Sunday lunchtime kick-off, with a large support from Leeds once again heading to Wigan. I surpassed myself this morning by forgetting we were leaving Leeds at 9am; the realisation hit as we were getting ready to leave the house at 7am! As my daughter Dani had stayed the night, we both could have done with an extra hour's sleep.

I felt there had been a lot in the news this week about Leeds; firstly the news that Berardi will be out for 16 weeks with a hamstring tendon rupture that will heal without surgery. He must be gutted to be out with another bad long-term injury. We also had little Freddie Callaghan from Ireland making his appearance on *Soccer AM* dressed at Marcelo Bielsa, and well done to him. When I first saw his photo appear on Twitter showing him dressed like that for Halloween, I couldn't get over the likeness to Bielsa! A further thing has been the 'Sky TV are f***ing s**t' chant which has found itself in the news this week. As many of us have long suspected, our chants are muted when televised, which wouldn't be so bad if it was just these chants, not that I sing it personally. When our fans are on song, the atmosphere is out of this world and should not be muted so our worldwide fans can join in with us. There had been a 'debate' amongst Leeds fans, if you can call it that, on one of the Facebook groups I frequent. The owner of the first comment posted that

Leeds fans were hypocritical for singing that when they will have Sky at home. Another said that it affects the travelling support, especially our long-distance fans, who have to change their travel arrangements which costs them money – his answer was that they still have three weeks before the game to make a booking. As pointed out to him, fans book early to get the cheapest prices they can, and also once they have got a ticket they need to have their travel arrangements sorted. Unfortunately, there was no getting through to him, so I left it that the fans who sing it are entitled to their opinion whether they have Sky or not!

I would like to say a big thank you to John for buying all five of my books today, so happy reading and I look forward to getting feedback in due course. Evie was made up after buying my first book *Follow Me and Leeds United* then having her photo taken, so thank you once again. Just a reminder that autographed copies of all my books are available through me at any game. *Follow Me and Leeds United, Once a Leeds fan, always a Leeds fan, The Sleeping Giant Awakens, Leeds United 2016-17 and Back to Reality, Leeds United 2017-18* are all priced at £12.99. *The Good, The Bad and The Ugly of Leeds United, Leeds United in the 1980s* is £14.99. As Christmas is coming, don't forget these will make great presents for the Leeds United fan in your life. With lots of recollections from my early days of following Leeds, to the latter two books depicting the last two seasons travelling home and away with Leeds, there are plenty of stories that will resonate with our great support. With lots of photos in them, you may even find yourself in one! Our stop today was in Leyland again, which was packed with Leeds fans plus a few Man City ones, before we made our way to the ground. I was to meet Phil Thumbsup Cresswell there, who was buying my new book, so thank you to him for the support.

The team: Peacock-Farrell, Douglas (back from injury), Dallas at right-back, Cooper, Jansson, Philips, Roofe, Forshaw, Alioski, Hernandez and Klich. Subs: Shackleton for Klich (90+1). Attendance was 14,799, with 4,856 Leeds fans. Leeds won the game 2-1, with goals from Hernandez (9) and Roofe (46).

By the time we reached the ground it was 1pm and luckily although there was plenty of traffic, we didn't get caught on the gridlocked roads after an earlier car crash next to the ground which the team got caught up in. By the time we'd walked to the ground, put my flag up and walked to where Dani's seat was, I didn't realise the teams were out on the pitch and ready for the minute's silence. This was for both Armistice Day and the Leicester City owner and staff who were killed in a helicopter crash leaving their stadium last week. The silence was immaculately observed in the stands, but underneath on the concourse no one was aware it was taking place.

With Wigan unbeaten at home so far this season, I was hoping that for once we could turn that stat around. We'd had a conversation in the pub about Dallas playing at right-back. I didn't like him playing in that position but I said I would be happy for him to prove me wrong. As my friend Sue said, she thought it was more about him moving forward than the defensive part and I hadn't thought about that. As it was, I thought he had a good game today.

Within six minutes of the start, we found ourselves a goal down after Wigan were awarded a free kick just outside the area. Despite it taking ages before the kick was taken, the ball was kicked into the right-hand side of the net, opposite us. I thought if we'd have had someone on both posts for set pieces and corners, it would make it harder for the opposition to score. Once again we'd given ourselves an uphill battle at the start of the game. For once, though, within three minutes we had equalised with a fantastic move that saw Klich asking for the ball in open space, pass the ball across the goal, where Hernandez was there to stick it in to the net right in front of us. Sending the Leeds support into raptures was certainly true, as the lads behind kept falling into me. I was trying to keep on my feet to get some photos, which proved difficult, but celebrations have to be done! With that, loads of Leeds fans started coming out of the stand to our right and were brought into ours. This upset some Wigan fans, who didn't like the fact we'd had loads of fans in their stand too. We had a couple of great chances, but their goalkeeper was on hand to palm the ball away. We had lots of possession from then on and Wigan weren't in the game very much. They had small pockets of attack, but I thought we coped with the game very well as we went in at half-time 1-1.

I took a few photos of fans beneath the stands and had a chat with Tina and Kev before going back to my seat. As I got to the top of the stairs, I said, 'when did the teams come back out?' as that seemed to have been a quick half-time. With that, the ball was passed across the goal by Hernandez, and with Roofe bearing down on their keeper, whose defender got in the way, he got the loose ball and stuck it into an empty net. That was a welcome goal, with many fans missing it as they were still down below the stands. I headed back to my seat and, in the middle of taking one photo, nearly jumped out of my skin as someone let one of those 'bomb fireworks' go off in the seats to my left, close to where Dani was. I'm sorry but I won't agree these should be at a game and I wish those who bring them into the stands wouldn't do it. I know this will fall on deaf ears though, sadly. We came close to scoring again and the Leeds fans were in good voice, as they had been for most of the game. With Wigan fans resorting to a drum to whip up any atmosphere, they were pretty poor to be honest. When all their fans stood up and started clapping, I had no idea what it was for as I hadn't seen anything on social media beforehand. As I tried to clap too, no Leeds fans joined in so I gave up. I saw something mentioned later about Dave Whelan, their owner, so need to read up on that as I assumed that is who it was for. The lads in front of me were going mad as a woman in front of them had not taken any interest in the game and spent the whole 90 minutes playing games on her phone. I found it very strange to be honest, unless she'd attended under duress, but, with tickets being sold out in minutes, if you don't want to watch the game there are plenty of fans who do.

After having some strange decisions made by the officials, plus heavy tackles flying in left, right and centre from Wigan, it was good to see one of them booked. The longer teams get away with fouls, the more they do. A couple of times Wigan attacked and it looked like they had got the better of our defence, but one thing that shone out is the fact that our players play as a team. With

about six of our players bearing down on their attacker, we got the better of him and then started another attack once more. With Shackleton being the only sub today at the start of five minutes of injury time, he was unlucky not to score. As I headed to get my flag, one lad shouted, 'Heidi where are you going?' My response was to go and get my flag, so that was alright lol! The Leeds fans were singing, 'we're Leeds United, we're top of the league'. I couldn't sing it until the final whistle blew so as not to jeopardise anything, and it was a relief to hear the whistle blow for full time. We broke another stat as this was the first game since Boxing Day when the opposition had scored first and we ended up winning, so well done lads.

As a very happy support came out of the ground, we got to the coach and were soon on our way. Stuck in traffic, our coach kept stalling so our driver turned right up a road, and it was only as we got to the top of it that we realised we weren't going any further. With no power at all, we couldn't get the coach onto the main road. I said would it help if we pushed the coach, to which the driver said yes that would be a good idea. With that, a dozen of us got out and started to push the coach from behind. Although I managed to get a couple of photos, I did push it too, despite getting accused of just taking photos lol! It certainly did the trick as we got the coach over the incline and set off. I thought it was going to mean no Sunday tea at my elder daughters for us, but luckily we made it back to Leeds in one piece. I'd been asleep when we'd passed a crash on the motorway, so hopefully no one was hurt in it.

It felt good to get a win today and next week sees us head to West Bromwich Albion for the first time in a long while for another evening kick-off. There are plenty of tales from our times at their ground, with one in my first book being Jonny Giles's testimonial, which a group of us attended in the 70s. When lads with Brummie accents pretended to be Leeds fans then showed their true credentials, it turned out to be a bad night for my friends and I! I don't think that'll happen when we visit them next week!

WEST BROMWICH ALBION (A) – 10 NOVEMBER 2018

It was a 5.30pm kick-off that beckoned today but things got off to a bad start when the coaches didn't turn up on time due to a mix up. I was on coach two today, but as coach one got ready to go with our driver from last week, there were reminisces from then when it wouldn't go! Eventually it did so instead of leaving at 12pm we were at least 40 minutes late. Our pub stop in Sutton Coldfield was reduced to 90 minutes, where Worksop and Harrogate Whites had stopped too.

It was a long time since I'd visited the Hawthorns and can't really remember when I was last there. Games I can remember were Johnny Giles's testimonial game and also Telford in the FA Cup. I wasn't there when we were relegated as for two years I only went to home games due to having my first two children. What I can remember though from our early visits were scores of Leeds fans getting arrested for nothing. Even when we scored and were cheering when we scored a goal that was the excuse to wade into our fans on the terraces and drag anyone out.

One thing that happened this week corroborated one of my stories in my first book *Follow Me and Leeds United*. A newspaper cutting shared on my timeline from John Murgatroyd in Harrogate confirmed what I'd written in the book. As I've said many a time, everything I've written about is true, there is nothing made up and even though it has taken 47 years for it to be confirmed, I wasn't far off!

'Abbey Coachways ran a coach to the matches at Coventry and Nottingham in 1971. At Nottingham I wore a six-foot scarf that I had made. I was quite naïve to the fact that there may be trouble at matches at this stage. We were followed into Nottingham by a couple of Wallace Arnold coaches. These coaches had a middle door as well as one at the front, and Leeds fans kept opening this door and hanging out of the coach. Going back to the coach after the match, I hid my scarf under my coat, with a bit of difficulty I might add, and probably looked six months pregnant! As I was going across the bridge over the River Trent I was in the middle of all the Forest boot boys who were looking for Leeds fans. It was the first time I had really seen anything like this but I was laughing to myself as I was a Leeds fan in the middle of them and they didn't know it. Once back on the coach, I began to hear stories from the other fans on my coach about the escapes they'd had. We heard that a Leeds fan had been forced to swim the Trent and another had been stabbed in the back and collapsed onto the steps of a Wallace Arnold coach. How true these stories were can only be confirmed by people who were involved.'

We got to the ground in plenty of time for kick-off, but as there was no space for my flag as they wouldn't let Leeds fans put them at the front due to advertising rights, I left mine in my bag. Before the game started, and with the 100th anniversary of the end of the First World War tomorrow, the *Last Post* was played and an immaculately observed minute's silence took place.

The team: Peacock-Farrell, Dallas, Alioski, Cooper, Jansson, Douglas, Phillips, Klich, Roofe, Forshaw and Hernandez. Subs: Roberts for Roofe (66), Harrison for Douglas (73), and Saiz for Klich (78). Attendance was 25,661, with 2,737 Leeds fans. Leeds lost the game 4-1, with Hernandez scoring a late consolation goal (90+2).

I didn't know what to expect from the game as I didn't know anything about them apart from them getting relegated last season, including forgetting that Bartley now played for them. As they mentioned he was out injured the realisation hit me. We were under the cosh from the word go, so I knew we weren't in for an easy game and expected them to raise their game as they were playing us. We had a few narrow escapes and Peacock-Farrell was forced into making a good save to stop them from scoring. We had plenty of possession but we didn't actually do anything with it. No one seemed to want to take charge in midfield, and I know we try patient build-ups but we kept giving silly passes away and that gave WBA the impetus to attack us. I was happy to get to half-time with the score 0-0 and it ended up with the Leeds fans still singing and it being very quiet from the home fans.

I went downstairs at half-time as I was hoping to see the Thames Valley Whites with their new flag, which was a tribute to the fallen and Armistice Day, but sadly I never found them. Speaking to a friend of mine at half-time, she said beware of the pavements around West Brom as they jump up and hit you in the face! Things got quite scary as we were trying to get back to our seats at the end of half-time. Stewards were blocking the tops of the stairs and wouldn't let anyone back up in to the stand. As more and more fans came up behind us and we started to get crushed, things could so easily have got out of hand, with things kicking off when there was no need at all. Luckily, they soon saw sense and let us up, but that was stupid and irresponsible.

It turned out to be a tale of two halves because within six minutes we were a goal down. From having a penalty appeal turned down, the ball ended up with their player taking on two of ours, who hesitated, looking for an offside flag. This was when I realised how strong and big some of their players were. Unfortunately they went on to score. What we had been doing was trying to walk the ball into the net instead of shooting, which meant we had very few on target. We did get into a couple of good positions but our shots were wide. For those fans involved, keeping the ball is counterproductive, especially as we were losing. Within a few minutes from this, with misplaced passes from us and WBA getting the rub of the green, with the ball running in their favour more often than not, they scored again. It did look like Peacock-Farrell was going to save it, but unfortunately it looked to go through his hands for their second. I still thought we could get something from the game at that point, even though we didn't really look like scoring. When the

ball ricocheted off one of our players straight to theirs to run on and score, it was game over. It wasn't the end though as WBA got a fourth and we were down and out! With that, the Leeds fans came into their own once again and showed what makes me love our support. Those left behind did a great rendition of 'We all love Leeds' over and over again, which made Hernandez chip the ball over their keeper to pull one back, although too little, too late. As the Leeds fans carried on with the song even after the final whistle, it meant some of our players came straight over to clap us all. As always I'm proud to be a Leeds fan. As I came down the steps and met my daughter Dani, she said when Hernandez scored she was the only one where her seat was just behind the goal, as gaps had appeared all around her when their fourth went in.

There was something kicking off downstairs with the police surrounding some Leeds fans and one lad in particular. Eventually, it looked like things had calmed down as he walked past us but then no end of coppers followed him as we carried on past. As we got to the bottom of the walkway and ready to cross the road, some police were getting high and mighty with some Leeds fans, although I'd not seen or heard anything out of order. I tried to diffuse the situation for some lads and one said it was his brother with them, but the police were being heavy handed when there was no need. I got the lad away and I know he was angry about being pushed around and wanted the number of the person who had pushed him. Unfortunately, knowing how bad they could be down there, I said it wasn't worth him getting done for it no matter how angry he was. He did thank us though. Someone said they knew what was wrong with Leeds: too much breastfeeding,

119

although I think sleepless nights would be true! I had to laugh at that because with four or five newborn babies within the last few weeks, our players' wives did all the work to begin with! I had some fans blaming Peacock-Farrell for letting the goals in though, but I didn't agree. Maybe he should have got the second but it was individual errors and bad passing further up the field that caused them to counter attack. Our failings of not shooting further out and trying to walk the ball into the net proved costly today in my opinion. Hearing Mick Hewitt had taken one of his branch members to hospital today, I hope they are okay and get well soon.

Back to the drawing board for us today, and back to reality as we were taught a lesson in that second half. It was men against the boys but ex-premiership money showed. Whilst I don't want to go back to silly money for players, there was nobody on the bench who was going to come on and be a match for them in those stakes. With another international break upon us, there is no game next week before we return to Elland Road for the Bristol City game. With the rugby game at Elland Road tomorrow, I only hope they don't damage the pitch, and that is one reason why I don't like them having their games at our ground.

Thank you to Jan, Carl, Daniel, Daz and the Masons for buying my new book *Back to Reality*. Your support is appreciated, plus a thank you to those of you who took the time to say you enjoy reading my books and my blog. Speaking of my blog, to hear it has gone as far as China courtesy of Charley from Harrogate is good to hear and again thanks to him and anyone else who shares my blogs with others.

BRISTOL CITY (H) – 24 NOVEMBER 2018

After a week of feeling up and down and lacking in get up and go, I was woken by my youngest granddaughter Alexis, age four, Facetiming me and asking if she could come to the football instead of Laura. Well that melted my heart and jolted me into action. It's surprising what a little bit of love can do! I was unable to attend the funeral of our oldest Leeds United fan Edna Newton yesterday, but heard she got a great send off with lots of Leeds fans turning up as well as her family. There was also a lovely touch from the club who sent their own wreath, which was placed at Billy's statue after her funeral. With Bremner Square around Billy's statue now even larger with more stones in place, we headed there straight away and it looks fantastic, with lots of memories for so many fans now. It was nice to meet up with some fans from the Isle of Man there who regularly read my blogs, and they will now have their photo in this one.

On our way to the Peacock, I remembered that someone from work wanted a programme as her dad should be in it. On stopping at Phil Beeton's cabin, we bumped into some of our Norwegian fans who had come over for the game. When I took a photo, I hadn't realised at that time it was Phil's birthday. I hope he enjoys reading my new book *Back to Reality, Leeds United season 2017-18* that his wife Chris brought for him as a surprise. I'd had a great surprise during the week when my neighbour Keith had brought ten of the same book at once. When Tony came up to me as I passed him on Lowfields Road later, he said 'guess what I got for my birthday?' His son had bought two of my books for him. As usual my grateful thanks go to them for their support. I also caught up with Simon plus some more of our Norwegian fans and Jørn from Denmark in the Peacock.

Leeds had sold out all the tickets for the home support once again for this game. After the international break last weekend, it felt like ages since we'd played. With more serious injuries for members of our squad with the broken leg for Blackman plus Jansson and Peacock-Farrell being out, this meant a couple of our youngsters coming into the team today.

The team: Will Huffer in goal for his debut, Cooper, Phillips, Dallas, Alioski, Roofe, Forshaw, Klich, Douglas, Aapo Halme, making his first appearance at centre-back, and Hernandez. Subs: Harrison for Alioski (61), Saiz for Halme (64) and Baker for Klich (82). Leeds won 2-0, with goals from Roofe (69) and Hernandez (86). Attendance was 34,333, with 889 Bristol City fans.

Someone had asked me how I thought we'd play and I said I'd no idea but needed a win. The good thing about Huffer being in goal was that the whole squad, including the under 23s, were all trying to play the same game, so he should be fine. The first half saw Leeds have a lot of possession but the one thing that wasn't happening were shots on goal. Their keeper, to begin with, looked very shaky and I felt that we needed to put him under pressure. Although the game was at a steady pace, I didn't think Bristol offered too much, although they had a good chance when the ball came to one of their players on the edge of the area but his shot was wayward. We'd had a shot on target and should have done better, with at least a couple more. The two young debutants were playing well, doing what they had to do and playing it safe despite a couple of hairy moments. Bristol had a couple of patches putting us under pressure but I thought we coped with them very well. My only fear was that déja vu moment of us having lots of the ball and them breaking away to score, but the score was even as we went in to the break.

The second half started off as it had been left at the end of the first half. I felt that we needed to freshen things up at that time, but then the Leeds fans came into their own once more and became the 12th man. The South Stand started with the Klich song *It could be 20 yards or 30 yards, everywhere we go, 40 yards or 50 yards, Klich is scoring goals, Klich is scoring goals!* With the Kop joining in, this upped the atmosphere and had an immediate effect on the players. Not long after, their player fouled Roofe in the middle of the park and got a deserved booking. The next thing I saw was the red card out as he was sent off. I hadn't realised he'd already been booked and, despite his manager saying at the end of the game that the ref had been swayed by the crowd, he deserved to go. The ref had been almost invisible for a lot of the game because for once he let the game flow a lot, well most of the time! The team upped the tempo and then Bielsa made two subs within a few minutes of each other, with Harrison and then Saiz coming on. As someone shouted 'we can't keep trying to walk the ball into the net', it wasn't long before we got the goal to put us into a well-deserved lead when Roofe scored from close range. At that time I didn't expect us to do anything else but win the game. We had a lot of pressure

but then Bristol had a spell where they won a couple of corners and attacked us. I didn't feel worried though because we dealt with the threats before taking the impetus again. After Saiz put a great cross in for Hernandez to head the ball into the net for our second goal, that was it – game over. A win and three points were gratefully received – thank you.

When the subs were being made earlier, I've no idea what was happening with the person putting the numbers up. On one of my photos Bielsa looks to be angry about something so no doubt we'll find out in due course. On to our second home game in a few days when we play Reading on Tuesday. Whether any of our injured players come back by then I don't know, but I'm sure our youngsters will fit in just fine.

READING (H) – 27 NOVEMBER 2018

For those waiting to read my blog, apologies that it's taken so long to post this.

On arrival at Elland Road after a miserable wet journey, we went to the club shop via the food bank. My granddaughter Hannah had received her runners-up prize from the Leeds United Supporters' Trust after their recent competition and was itching to spend her vouchers. They didn't last long as she came out with a new Leeds United hoodie, so thank you for the prize as it was greatly appreciated by a happy little girl. As we stood chatting to my sister Erica and Carol, some of our Norwegian and Danish fans arrived so we had plenty to talk about and more photos taken. Also, one of our Welsh contingent arrived and it was disappointing to hear that, despite not having missed a game for three years, he had missed out on Bolton tickets. I'm not sure what has happened when we get large allocations, but I was told recently that the away season-ticket holders get priority, and then there was supposed to be a small allocation for those with most loyalty before the free for all. I know you can't please everyone, but the club must look after loyal supporters. It's fine when things are on the up but if – and fingers crossed they won't – things take a turn for the worse again, then it is the ones who stay through thick and thin who will be there. That doesn't take anything away from those who can only come and go as their circumstances allow, as I don't decry any of our support. My niece Sonya arrived with her Methley teammates for their photo just before we went into the ground.

The team: Peacock-Farrell (back after injury), Cooper, Phillips, Douglas, Hernandez, Alioski, Baker, Roofe, Klich, Dallas and Forshaw. Subs: Saiz for Baker, Clarke for Alioski (46) and Shackleton for Klich (73). Leeds won the game 1-0, with Dallas scoring our goal (60). Attendance was 27,806, with 197 Reading fans.

I knew there weren't many Reading fans there but was surprised to see there were so few. I see the Leeds fans didn't turn up because Reading ultras were coming according to Twitter lol!! Although we started off on the attack, we had Peacock-Farrell to thank for tipping the ball over the crossbar to prevent Reading taking the lead. The first half didn't set the ground alight as most things petered out and things became very silent on the terraces. What little did happen meant that

I couldn't wait for half-time to come, as did many others by the looks of it.

Bielsa changed things at the start of the second half, making a double substitution with Saiz and Clarke coming on. Young Clarke had an immediate impact, running down the left-hand side to us on the Kop, and we were very unlucky not to take the lead. This immediately upped both the tempo on the pitch and the atmosphere on the terraces, a real tale of two halves. When we'd come close a couple of times I said a goal would come and it certainly did, courtesy of Dallas, who at the time had started to play very well. Their goalie had made an initial save but Dallas pounced to put the ball into the net to the joy and relief of the Leeds fans. On the up, we came very close to getting a second after more great work from Clarke. After that, Peacock-Farrell was called on to make another great save as Reading didn't give up and started to attack us more. We didn't give up either as play switched to our end again and Roofe was denied by their keeper after Clarke put a great pass into the box again. Just when we thought we could see the game out, there was a penalty shout but not in our favour, surprise, surprise. No it was given to Reading, as I shouted to Peacock-Farrell to save it. Well he certainly did and what a fantastic save it was! The difference between a draw and a win as we took the three points, sending all the Leeds fans home happy having seen two wins in a row at Elland Road.

Saturday sees us head to Sheffield Utd for another early kick-off and another game on Sky. We are going straight there for this one so at least it's not too early a start for us.

CHAPTER 6

SHEFFIELD UNITED (A) – 1 DECEMBER 2018

We caught the coach at Elland Road on another miserable and wet day to head to the lunchtime kick-off that had been put back 30 minutes for Sky. Having just read on Twitter that a Leeds fan had arrived at the ground saying it was very quiet, we couldn't help laughing when it turned out they were at Hillsborough, oops! Our coach driver then forgot to pull off on one junction of the M1 to pick some of our fans up so we had a detour. On hearing some trains were also delayed I hoped that was the end of things going wrong. Luckily, we were still in the first group of coaches who got escorted to the ground for the relatively short journey.

As we got off the coach and headed back to the shop for a Costa, loads and loads of riot police were arriving and it felt very intimidating but also way over the top. As we passed the turnstiles someone with a camera turned to point it at us as we went by but I've no idea who it was. If I thought the silly things had finished happening they hadn't, but as usual I think I surpassed that. As we made our way to the front of the stand, I told the stewards I was going to put my flag at the front. Wrong! I stood there as it dawned on me that the reason my bag felt lighter was because I'd taken it out for our home games as it only goes to away games! I couldn't believe I'd been so stupid, but never mind I got photos of the rest that were displayed, including the Remembrance one put there by one of the Thames Valley Whites. I have to say it is absolutely beautiful. I then heard someone had left their ticket at home too and had to ask for a duplicate to be picked up at the ground. With that I said we'd had our fair share of things not going our way so things can only get better, especially as we hadn't won here since 1992. There were some Argentinian fans here due to the Bielsa effect so I took photos of them too. I took a photo of the Sheff Utd mascot who then indicated he wanted a photo with me. With that, I think it was our photographer who raced over to get a photo too.

The team: Peacock-Farrell, Jansson (back after injury), Cooper, Phillips, Douglas, Hernandez, Alioski, Roofe, Klich, Dallas and Forshaw. Subs: Halme for Cooper (went off with a serious injury) (21), Clarke for Alioski (46) and Shackleton for Hernandez (90). Leeds won the game 1-0, with Hernandez scoring our goal (82). Attendance was 25,794, with 2,243 Leeds fans.

Jansson returned to the defence for the game after his recent injury. At least we didn't have a repeat of last season when we were a goal down within a couple of minutes. Things were fairly even to begin with, although I couldn't help noticing they had a couple of giant players who were able to bully us off the ball. A couple of times they managed to come straight through the middle to attack us and, I can't remember who, but one of our players tussled with a Sheffield player to win the ball. Cooper, behind them, went down and I didn't think he'd been involved in the tussle, but I knew he was in trouble when he hit the ground in frustration. What surprised me was seeing him limping off between two of our trainers. With how bad he looked, I thought they'd carry him off but they didn't. Young Halme came on and he got involved straight away. I felt that by having his debut recently, that had helped him because his maturity today showed immensely in my opinion. Apart from one header that put us under pressure and brought a great save out of Peacock-Farrell in the second half, I didn't think he put a foot wrong, which was great to see. Before half-time Sheff Utd did put us under pressure and come close to scoring but we ended the half on the upper foot. Our passing was causing lots of frustration for them with some bad fouls which resulted in deserved bookings for them.

Alioski had been replaced by Clarke again at the start of the second half. The one thing that I'd noticed about Alioski was him sticking close to one of their giants, and although he was bullied a lot it looked like he was frustrating their player. He was also standing at one or the other of the goal posts when we were defending corners, so I'm glad to see my rants about not having anyone on the line have been listened to lol! The second half seemed to start quietly for us and it was a shame we'd had to stop for the break when we were on the up. Sheff Utd also started to attack us again but my thoughts were that they'd start off well and then calm down again. At that time I thought Bielsa needed to change things, but when he didn't my instincts were that he knew what he was doing and I had to trust his judgement. We started getting on top and when a great cross was put across the box it was a shame it didn't result in a goal. The linesman to the left of us needed to borrow my glasses as he didn't seem to be able to tell when a ball was in or out. With one that gave

us an advantage when I'm sure it was out, it would have been a case of poetic justice for once if it had resulted in a goal. We eventually did get that breakthrough when Clarke chased their keeper, who took one step too far. Clarke won the ball, passed it to Hernandez in acres of space in the middle, who slammed the ball into the net to send everyone wild in the stand behind the goal. We came under pressure in the last few minutes but were able to see the game out and get the win, to the delight of the Leeds fans. My daughter Dani said there were some Leeds fans to the left of the stand we were in who came down doing the Leeds salute. I love the fact that we will always know who our fans are!

As I waited for Dani to come out of the stand, Steph passed me and told me I wasn't allowed to bring my flag anymore, and Paul also said the same thing to me outside too. Some lads said, 'we need to get a photo; this is from the Leeds 1919 site.' As we got back on the coach someone shouted that we had to sit at the back of the coach again next time, which we'd had to do, as someone had already been in our regular seats. I'm not sure if we've been relegated or promoted to the back, but all these superstitions were seen coming out again today. Old habits die hard I'm afraid as a Leeds fan. We were back in Leeds in no time and I had another detour to make to Guiseley to a family 18th party before getting home. I'm sure we will have another full house against QPR at Elland Road now, especially as we had a brief spot of being top of the league before Norwich snatched it back off us. It is very tight at the top but as I've said before, anyone can beat anyone in this division. We just need to keep up there with the others challenging and see where we are in the coming months. Just get as many points as we can and who knows at this point where we will be.

QPR (H) – 8 DECEMBER 2018

Yesterday was a poignant day for Leeds United fans with the 21st anniversary of the death of my hero Billy Bremner. My thoughts were also with his family as often we forget that as well as a footballer, he was also a dad and a husband. I'd also seen a photo I'd taken at Brighton a couple of seasons ago appear on my timeline thanking me for taking it. Sadly one of the Leeds fans in the photo died this week, but I'm glad I was able to capture the photo with some happy memories. RIP Gary. Unfortunately, after making plans to go to The Duncan today for the unveiling of the plaques in memory of Chris and Kev, I had to change my plans after a 16-hour day yesterday looking after family. Sadly you can't always do what you want to do as I was looking forward to recording it all. I've heard, though, that it was rammed and everything went well so I'm glad to hear that.

With another storm around with heavy winds and rain, we arrived at Elland Road to see a rainbow, which at one point looked to be over the ground. After seeing two separate magpies then this, I thought it was Billy saying we would win today. With a visit to the Peacock first, there was a good atmosphere in there as the singing crew were in full voice. I have been asked to share the song words, which are below:

I've seen Leeds win the proper title

Under those shining diamond lights

I've seen us plough our way through Europe

I've seen us turn to f***ing shite

Go tell the mancs n scouse

Biesla's in our house

Leeds Utd on the rise

Go tell the mancs n scouse

Biesla's in our house

Leeds Utd on the rise

We got into the ground having missed all the showers but sadly those at the front of all the stands were very unlucky to avoid it during the game.

The team: Peacock-Farrell, Jansson, Douglas, Shackleton (first league start at Elland Road), Phillips, Roofe, Klich, Hernandez, Alioski, Saiz and Forshaw. Subs: Halme for Saiz (81) and Clarke for Hernandez (86). Leeds won the game 2-1, with Roofe scoring both our goals (45+3, 53 penalty), including the first penalty awarded to us since September 2017. Attendance was 33,781, with approximately 300 QPR fans.

I hadn't any preconceptions really about the game but it was good to see Saiz back in the side from the start. The crowd were in a jovial mood with plenty of singing. We had a couple of great chances in the opening minutes but failed to put the ball into the back of the net. We continued attacking and putting QPR under pressure before they broke away and brought a good save out of Peacock-Farrell. Then against the run of play QPR took the lead. From a bad pass and then the rub of the green twice when the ball ran in their favour, they got the better of Phillips and Jansson to put the ball into the net. For once I didn't think we'd go a goal down as we hadn't been playing badly. QPR time wasted so much it antagonised the crowd, but the referee didn't pull them up for it. When three minutes of injury time was put up I said, 'come on Leeds let's get a goal before half-time', although not with any conviction, so it took us all by surprise when we did get the equaliser just before the whistle went, which was very welcome especially with the timing of it.

At half-time it was nice to catch up with Trampas and I'd only just been talking about him to my friend Carole when he turned up. As I came back up into the stand the teams were already on the pitch and Leeds had started an attack towards the Kop. Our long wait for a penalty was finally over as their player handballed it. Roofe stepped up to take the kick and put it into the right corner of the goal from where we were stood in the Kop. He was unlucky not to get a hat-trick later on but the flag went up for offside and Klich brought a great save out of their keeper too. Although QPR put pressure on in the final moments, for once I wasn't too worried as I thought we were coping well with their attacks. We had Peacock-Farrell to thank for tipping the ball over the cross bar to keep them out though. We'd been too casual a couple of times which had caught us out, but

on the whole I thought we played well today and deserved the points. When some started singing we were top of the league, I said, 'nooo … don't sing that until the final whistle blows,' especially when someone said Norwich were losing. Well, of course, they scored in the last minute again to stay top. That said, anyone can beat anyone in this division and as long as we are picking points up and staying in the mix, that's all we need to do at the moment.

We were lucky going back to the car as the rain stopped again just in time, but the road outside McDonalds was completely flooded. Luckily the weather eased off on the way home, especially as I was heading straight out again with the other half. There was a fundraiser at Green Hammerton Club for the British Heart Foundation in memory of Leeds supporter Keith Horner, who died recently. Ian Smith, a Leeds fan, played Soul and Motown music from vinyl records and it was a great night, especially as just before we left *Marching on Together* and the *Ballad of Billy Bremner* were played in Keith's memory. See you next week at Bolton.

BOLTON (A) – 15 DECEMBER 2018

After telling someone on Thursday that I don't expect anyone to leave us in the January transfer window and also I wasn't going to count my chickens just yet as to where Leeds will finish at the end of the season, I came home to hear the news that Saiz was on his way. Things had been mooted a while ago that he wasn't happy but I was very disappointed to hear this. Later Moscow White, on Twitter, gave more insight into the decision and it looks like the club has been very supportive of them. It turns out his wife is due to give birth having already lost the twin of this due baby. Having had problems with the birth of their first daughter, including a cancer scare for mum around the same time, I can totally understand that being here instead of near their family in Spain would make them want to return home. As Saiz has a loan with a view to buy, who knows how this will pan out in the future. As someone who lost a baby tragically at 17 days old and having subsequent pregnancies, I can say that the fear of something going wrong never leaves you. Even now, the sheer panic that a child isn't just going to be ill but will die envelops me. Good luck to them all.

As we headed to Bolton who were at the bottom of the league and once again having money problems, with their players and staff being unpaid (not sure if that's been sorted as yet), for the life of me I couldn't understand why they hadn't given us more tickets? We'd sold out in minutes once again and last time they had been in trouble they gave us at least 7,000 tickets. Surely selling us more tickets could have immediately helped with their cash flow? Obviously not!

I went to Elland Road early as the weather forecast of snow and freezing rain, although not due till at least 10am in Halifax, meant I wanted to get there in time for the coach. Getting home after would sort itself out. I decided to look for a specific Bremner stone in the Lucas Radebe area. As I saw quite a few names I recognised, I took some photos then found my freezing fingers nearly dropped off!

We stopped off in Bury before the game and had a decent time there today. With the White Rose branch in too, I'd like to say a big thank you to Gary Noble for buying my latest book *Back to Reality,*

Leeds United 2017-18. As always I am grateful for the support. After hearing one of the barmaids saying she'd been in Valencia to see that red team over the Pennines, it reminded me of a tweet I'd seen this week. Outside the ground in Valencia had been painted — Scum free zone, a Leeds badge and a painted Hernandez portrait. On the day of the game, the red fans had complained so someone painted over the Scum free zone but left the rest. It was quite bizarre really.

As we got to the ground the weather had deteriorated as the rain came down. I had taken my flag with me today and put it up at the top of the stairwell, but, as a part of it came down, I retied it. After taking photos I headed to my seat for the start of the game.

The team: Peacock-Farrell, Phillips, Jansson, Hernandez (Captain), Shackleton, Roofe, Klich, Forshaw, Baker, Douglas and Alioski. Subs: Clarke for Baker (46), Bamford for Roofe (61) and Halme for Hernandez (90). Leeds won the game 1-0, with Bamford scoring five minutes after coming on (66). Attendance was 17,484, with 4,550 Leeds fans. Looking at the spaces on the Bolton terraces I found that attendance hard to believe to be honest.

As the game kicked off, Leeds immediately went on the attack and their goalkeeper prevented Leeds taking an early lead by tipping Hernandez's effort over the bar. We won plenty of corners in the opening part of the game and saw plenty of the ball. The ref kept the flow of the game going by playing on and not blowing his whistle for every challenge, which was good. We had quite a few misplaced passes but did look the better of the teams. Even though we had the majority of the game, with the rare attacks that Bolton had I was always wary that they would get a goal against the run of play. Shackleton was playing well, which was good to see. When I looked at my watch 36 minutes had already passed before the game petered out in the last minutes of the half as things quietened on the terraces. With the terrible conditions of driving rain on the pitch, it wasn't a surprise really.

I went downstairs, and as I was making my way back across the stand, all of a sudden, I smelt sulphur as we were nearly gassed out by a yellow flare or whatever they want to call it. It was awful as I struggled to breathe as I was full of cold. I'm sorry but I won't ever agree that it is right to let these things off in the middle of a crowd. There is no thought for any other fan caught up in it and should be knocked on the head, although I doubt it will be.

With Clarke brought on in place of Baker at the start of the second half, I was looking forward to a turn around. The atmosphere on the terraces picked up as Leeds went on the attack. It was good to see Clarke, with some great footwork, beating their players to put them under pressure. When Bamford was brought on as sub, I said that I hadn't been sure if he'd play with the atrocious conditions, but Bielsa will know what he's doing. Within five minutes the ball was in the back of the net in front of us, as Clarke had been involved first, the ball came across to Hernandez who did a nutmeg on their player and a first-time strike from Bamford was put into the net. I thought it was nice seeing Bamford race over to the bench and celebrate with, I thought, the trainers who'd helped him get over his recent injury.

Towards the end of the game, Bolton got into it more as they went in search of an equaliser. As their player went down in the penalty area my heart was in my mouth, but the ref said play on. I didn't realise they'd had one kicked off the line by Douglas as I'd gone to retrieve my flag before the end of the game. I'd tied it that many times to stop it falling down that it took me ages to untie it, although thanks to the lads who helped me on that score. In the last few minutes we seemed to be staying back and letting Bolton attack us, which I didn't like. It ended with Halme coming on to help us defend and keep the lead. Another three points and five out of five wins saw us go top of the league as Norwich were kicking off at 5.30pm. They ended up drawing by scoring another late goal, giving them a point, which meant we stayed top.

The journey back to Leeds saw really bad conditions on the roads so I was glad I wasn't driving at that point. We still had issues driving back home, with plenty of water standing, including ice in Halifax, but at least we got home safe and sound. Next Sunday is our last game before Christmas at Aston Villa. Just keep doing what we are doing and grinding out wins and see if we can end the year on a high.

ASTON VILLA (A) – 23 DECEMBER 2018

First of all, I want to wish the fantastic worldwide Leeds United supporters a very Merry Christmas and it's great to see us at the top of the league! Getting a last-minute winner today saw limbs everywhere and fantastic scenes in the away end, and long may it continue.

Last Wednesday I appeared on BBC Radio Leeds with Adam Pope on a Christmas wish special alongside a Bradford and Huddersfield fan. My wish was for Leeds to have some *inner strength* so we don't capitulate as we have in the past. I want us to continue doing what we are doing, getting as many points as we can and getting a good FA Cup run to keep the momentum going. Our good runs in the past came when we took games seriously in the cup.

On our way to the game today we stopped at a different pub in Sutton Coldfield where we received a good welcome from the landlady. Thanks to Brook and Neil and also Evie for buying my book *Back to Reality, 2017-18*. Thanks too to Will for buying *Once a Leeds fan, always a Leeds fan* and *The Good, The Bad and The Ugly of Leeds United, Leeds United in the 1980s*. One fella, in passing, said he'd give me a pound if we beat the Villa today and when I said 'only a pound?' he replied he was a pensioner. Just before we were getting ready to leave I got talking to some Villa fans. As I took their photo we were chatting and I mentioned my first visit to Villa to see Leeds play was a 0-0 League Cup game in the 70s, which ended with our coach coming under attack when stuck in traffic after the game. The barrage of bricks put all the windows bar one through and I had to get down in the aisle to protect myself. As they mentioned something about books, I told them I'd already written five. With that they moved over to one of the tables as I brought my books to show them. One of the lads said that he thought what I was doing writing the books and blogs were fantastic and says no one at Villa does that. Of all the years he'd been following Villa he has never taken any photos. I

said he should get together with others and write down those memories as it's important for fans to see how it really was following their team. As I was asked about the score today I said I wouldn't predict one as I always get it wrong. I want us to carry on as we are, keep getting points, and then see where we are. I also hoped it would be a good game and I wasn't worried about playing them. One of the Villa fans said that they could score goals but their defence and keeper were rubbish. It was nice to have some good-natured banter with their fans and the time passed so quickly that I didn't realise we were already due to leave.

We arrived at the ground in next to no time and my daughter Dani and I decided to go straight in rather than go down to the Witton pub. As we were stood talking to Brian from Wales, I suddenly saw the cameras pointing at us. Dani went 'not again mother, it's every time I'm with you!!' As I looked up they still had the camera pointed at us, then came nearer and the man was laughing. He said they were looking for Christmas jumpers and so got a close up of the Leeds badge on mine and then went. It was quite funny really.

The team: Peacock-Farrell, Jansson, Phillips, Ayling (back after injury), Roofe, Alioski, Klich, Forshaw, Harrison, Leif Davis (making his first-team debut at left-back after Douglas had to pull out of the game after the warm up due to illness) and Hernandez. Subs: Clarke for Harrison (45) and Shackleton for Davis (78). Leeds won 3-2 after Villa took an early two-goal lead, before goals from Clarke (56), Jansson (61) and Roofe (90+5) won the game for us. Attendance was 41,411, with approximately 2,500 Leeds fans.

We got off to the worst possible start when Villa took the lead within the first five minutes of the game. We had a chance to equalise when the ball was passed across the goal but we were unable to capitalise on it. To make matters worse, they got a second 12 minutes later to take a two-goal lead. Both goals had come from mistakes and at that time I thought we were in for a tough afternoon, although there was a pull on young Davis's shirt which was ignored for one of them. Villa looked strong as we tried to get some fluidity going to our football and we did get a couple more chances on target, but there wasn't enough power in our shots. We were unlucky not to have Villa score an own goal for us, but their keeper tipped the ball over the bar. I thought young Davis was playing really well, and although he was up against a skillful player he more or less matched him. It was good to see another of our youngsters coming into the team and not looking out of place. Just before half-time we won a free kick and I, along with many other Leeds fans, thought the ball had sailed into the net from Hernandez, but unfortunately for us it had gone wide.

As I was talking to Craig at half-time, he asked me if we were down and out. I said no because we'd had some chances, although we had not been powerful enough with our shots. His daughter Olivia had said it would be 4-3 to Leeds before the game.

The second half saw Clarke come on as sub and it didn't take us long to start having some impact on the game. It was high intensity and end-to-end play, before Clarke, attacking down the far side to our end, got the ball into the penalty area. I was trying to zoom back out to get a photo of the shot but missed it as the ball hit the back of the net. As the Leeds fans celebrated, Alioski got the ball back out of the net and everyone ran back to the centreline to get on with the game. Bielsa was just going to make a substitution but changed his mind then. We started to have so much of the play as we kept attacking, and as we won a corner a young kid ran on to the pitch doing the Leeds salute and put a stop to the momentum. Why would you risk getting banned but also stop play when we were losing? A few minutes later, though, Hernandez's corner was headed into the back of the net by Jansson to equalise as the Leeds support went wild again. Leeds were on a different level to the first half as they came forward to attack, again and again, and Klich had a shot saved to prevent us taking the lead. After another attack there was a shout for handball and a penalty, although we didn't get that. I will need to see it myself but others around me were adamant we should have had a penalty. With Alioski leading many of the attacks from the right, he was having a good game and his shot was parried by the keeper. Villa started to make a few attacks before Leeds kept the momentum going with counter attacks. With the final minutes of injury time, many fans had resigned themselves to a draw, which in itself would have been a good result. When Alioski crossed the ball, it was cleared only as far as Roofe, who slammed the ball into the net for the winner!

There were fantastic scenes of celebrations from the Leeds fans, with limbs everywhere. What a turnaround from two goals down; to get the win was absolutely fantastic, especially as it meant we went back to the top of the table. This is what is special about following Leeds, and long may it continue. I bumped into Craig and Olivia at the end of the game and he couldn't believe it, saying he was going to post *Heidi was right*! I said Olivia was too as she said we would win. It was a happy set of Leeds fans leaving the ground and the buzz amongst everyone was great. For once I'm going to enjoy Leeds being top of the league and we couldn't have asked for a better Christmas present. Today was a great advert for football with an end-to-end game, and other teams will, I'm sure, start taking notice of us. Having been live on Sky again today, they will have sat up and taken notice that the Sleeping Giant that was stirring a couple of years ago is now going up a notch under Bielsa. I also thought that maybe Saiz going was a blessing in disguise for Alioski, as he enjoyed so much of the play down the right-hand side today.

I'll spare a thought for friends who are going through a hard time health wise at this moment in time and any other Leeds fans too. Have a great Christmas everyone and see you at Elland Road on Boxing Day for another sell-out crowd.

BLACKBURN ROVERS (H) – 26 DECEMBER 2018

It's great to see that Santa brought some of my books for fans as presents. Kevin and his wife were attending the game today from Australia and I'd arranged to meet them in the Peacock pre-game. All five of my books were personally autographed so a big thank you to them for supporting me in purchasing them all at once. I also met up with Susan after the game for her Boxing Day present to

herself and also the lovely Bremner. Hopefully Bremner, wearing his special reindeer LUFC ears, can be seen on the photo. I look forward to receiving feedback from both Kevin and Susan in due course and hope they enjoy the read.

I woke up absolutely exhausted today, but as I'm tee-total I can't blame it on a hangover. A word of warning to myself for next year, don't try to take a plastic bung out of a bottle with scissors, which slipped then stabbed me in the hand. Secondly, don't put Cadbury's chocolates on the tree as half of them were devoured by my chocolate Labrador Maisie within 20 minutes of my back being turned. Luckily for us she's had no ill effects. Hopefully you've all had a great Christmas and things were calmer in your household than mine, or at least you didn't do silly things like I did!

After the fantastic last-minute win at Villa last Sunday, it certainly gave me a feel-good factor and put that extra spring in my step. The belief is there, but as we've been in this position before, I will not count my chickens just yet. Keep on doing what we are at the moment and see where we are sometime in the new year. With another sell-out home crowd, Elland Road was still buzzing with anticipation though.

The team: Peacock-Farrell, Jansson, Phillips, Ayling, Roofe, Alioski, Klich, Forshaw, Harrison, Douglas and Hernandez. Subs: Clarke for Harrison (60) and Shackleton for Ayling (69). Baker was due to come on as a sub again, but despite being stood on the side of the pitch he didn't actually make it on. Leeds won 3-2 in an enthralling finish once again after being behind 2-1 at the 90-minute mark. With four minutes of injury time on the clock, a brace from Roofe (90+1 and 90+4) won the game for us. An own goal by Williams (33) gave Leeds the lead in the first half. Attendance was 34,863, with 1,378 Blackburn fans.

The game set off at a blistering pace as Leeds took the game to Blackburn. Attacking the South Stand in the first half, we had loads of possession but that didn't stop Blackburn from trying to attack us. I've stopped panicking when we are passing the ball across the back, even when it gets too close for comfort. I said Leeds knew what they were doing as the lads in front of me were having the jitters. I know there will be times when we come unstuck but I'm sure we'll be fine in the long run. Alioski brought a fine save out of their keeper as we continued to attack their goal. Harrison was playing noticeably better than he did at Villa and it was his pass from the byline that was put into the net for an own goal to give us the lead around the half-hour mark. Alioski was unlucky to see his effort bounce back off the crossbar, which could have given us a comfortable two-goal lead at half-time but we had to settle for one instead. One thing that looked better today was our crossing from both wings into the penalty area.

By the time I got back up into the stand for the start of the second half, I realised it had already kicked off. As I heard the Blackburn fans singing, I did begin to wonder if they'd scored. As I reached my seat, the man at the end of our row said, 'What was that about?' as he explained Blackburn had been given a penalty and they'd equalised. That actually knocked the stuffing out of us for a while and the Leeds fans and team were really infuriated when shouts for hand ball were ignored by the ref. Now one of them was a definite hand ball because even I saw it! We did try to get the ball into the net, but their goalie was able to make saves from both Alioski and Klich and later denied Roofe. Jansson made a pin-point tackle at the last minute in the penalty area to deny Blackburn as they bore down on our goal. Luckily for us his long legs got there first to put the ball out for a corner just as it looked like they would score. When Blackburn were given a free kick outside the area it proved costly, as their player put the ball into the net for them to take the lead, despite Peacock-Farrell's attempts to save it. As their players celebrated like mad and had been time wasting prior to this, I know it was deflating to see them take the lead. Some fans left straight away after this but as usual I always stay until the bitter end. Wasn't I glad that I take that stance because for the second game running we ended up with fantastic scenes on the terraces after Roofe scored his first goal a minute into injury time to equalise for Leeds. Despite the heroics of their keeper he scored at the third attempt when the ball was deemed to have crossed the line. Just when you thought it couldn't get any better, I said to the man next to me that this was going in, repeatedly, and that's exactly what happened as delirious scenes overtook everyone on the terraces in celebration. Hernandez put the ball across for Roofe to head his second goal into the net for a fairytale ending to the game. Everyone was bouncing as I descended into tears of joy when the emotions overtook me big style. Believing we can do it is there, but it actually happening is another

thing, especially for those of us who have witnessed the doldrums of the last 15 years prior to this. Will this be our season when we finally return to the Premier League? We can only hope, but we can definitely enjoy the ride.

We return to Elland Road on Saturday for our last game of 2018 and our second home game in a week, for another 3pm kick-off against Hull. I'll admit, I had to check a few times that we were indeed kicking off at that time today as games are changed that much it felt totally unexpected. Keep going Leeds, and it was lovely seeing my granddaughter Hannah experience the special moments at the end of the game today. There will be plenty of other fans who have never experienced anything like it before, but I can assure you the feelings are out of this world. As we walked back to the car a Blackburn fan walked in front of us into car park A. We were chatting excitedly about the game with some fans as he shouted 'f**k you Leeds'. I shouted at him to stop being a bad loser as there was no need at all.

HULL CITY (H) – 29 DECEMBER 2018

I'd lost track of the days over the Christmas period and once again had to check the kick-off time. I couldn't believe there'd been three 3pm kick-offs in a week for us, which is unheard of, well it seems that way! My granddaughter Alexis and I went to the Pavilion first as we were meeting Marc Bracha, his son Frankie and friend Shaun from Norwich for a photo. Marc is the author of *Bairdy's Gonna Get Ya!* and it was good to catch up. We met when I was writing my third book with Andrew Dalton, *The Good, The Bad and The Ugly of Leeds United, Leeds United in the 1980s*. Marc's dad lives in Cyprus and is an avid reader of my blog so he will enjoy seeing their photo in it. After a quick visit to the Peacock, where I took a photo of a group of lads including one who had come from Thailand for the game, we headed into the ground. There was another sell-out crowd for Leeds fans for our last game of 2018. As the game kicked off, my superstitious nature took over when Leeds fans started singing we were top of the league. I just wanted to shush everyone and tell them not to sing it so as not to jinx the result!

The team: Peacock-Farrell, Ayling, Douglas, Phillips, Jansson, Klich, Forshaw, Hernandez, Roofe, Alioski and Harrison. Subs: Clarke for Harrison (45), Roberts for Douglas (64) and Shackleton for Ayling (77). Leeds lost the game 2-0. Attendance was 35,754, with 2,145 Hull fans.

It didn't take long to realise that we were up against a team that were going to cause us problems today. They were strong and fast but in the opening minutes kept getting free kicks given, which in my opinion, always makes teams go from strength to strength. One of their players was heading for the floor even before our player got near him and the ball! They were running at us on the break and caught us out a few times as they weaved in and out of our players. One of our downfalls was the fact we had numerous bad passes from different players across the pitch. We had a couple of chances but didn't put their keeper under any pressure before Hull took the lead 25 minutes into the game. We failed to clear the ball by trying to play our way out from the goalmouth when for once we should have got rid of it. Their goalkeeper made a good save before the break to deny us an equaliser from Hernandez.

The second half saw Harrison taken off and Clarke replacing him again. Unfortunately Harrison has failed to impress so far this season when given the chance to play. The second half saw Leeds trying to take the game to Hull, but once again we were caught out with their speed as they took advantage of our attack. Their counter attack saw them coast past Douglas, and although Peacock-Farrell was able to save their first shot unfortunately he'd no chance with the rebound. I felt we were lacking in midfield today as the Hull players seemed to bypass us with ease. Once Clarke came on, though, Hernandez seemed to up his game, although he was guilty of bad passing at times. Although Hull had got two goals, we hadn't given up as we attacked towards the Kop. Their goalie led a charmed life, making some great saves to deny us and we also had the ball kicked off the line at least twice, with him beaten. Roberts was unlucky not to score when the ball was cleared off the line. Hull were time wasting when making their subs and should have been brought to task by the referee. Unfortunately, he waited until Jansson intervened and then decided to book their player once he was off the pitch for his reaction, before booking Jansson too. He could have nipped that in the bud but decided not to! In injury time they resorted to more time-wasting tactics when their player went down in the penalty area and the game was stopped. It felt like we were never going to score today in our first defeat in eight games. A defeat was always going to happen sometime and despite the bad passing we did have chances to score as we did end the game on the attack.

Despite the defeat we were still going to be top of the table going into the new year. Norwich were winning, or so we thought, and it wasn't until we were back at the car that we realised they'd lost, so the result went in our favour. Forest away on New Year's Day is our next game so we will just have to pick ourselves up and get on with it. Happy New Year to Leeds fans everywhere and I look forward to seeing what 2019 brings for Leeds United as we head towards our centenary year.

CHAPTER 7

NOTTINGHAM FOREST (A) – 1 JANUARY 2019

I hope everyone had a Happy New Year and my wish is for Leeds United to keep fighting and see where we are in a couple of months in our quest for promotion. The saying that you never know what is around the corner is certainly true. As my family faces a challenging year ahead, what I will say is make the most of everything in front of you when you can. I won't go into too much detail on here, but I thank both Phillip Thumbsup Cresswell and Gary Edwards for their kind words which are greatly appreciated.

After a stop in Mansfield before the game we arrived in plenty of time for kick-off. After putting my flag up at the front of the stand it was nice to see Nikki and Rita, her guide dog, who is our honorary Leeds United fan. My daughter Danielle and I went downstairs then and a big thank you to Gary for buying my book *Back to Reality, Leeds United 2017-18*. As always I am grateful for the support of fans who buy my books. After taking photos of fans, we made our way to our seats in different parts of the stand. I saw some people getting escorted across the front of our stand and I thought they must be some of the players coming to join us. It turned out that I was right and Danielle was sat near them. Berardi, Cooper, Dallas and a couple more were sat at the front.

The team: Peacock-Farrell, Ayling, Douglas, Phillips, Jansson, Hernandez, Roofe, Alioski, Klich, Forshaw and Harrison. Subs: Clarke for Harrison (46) and Roberts for Douglas (78). Leeds lost the game 4-2, with Clarke (52) and Alioski (64) scoring our goals. Attendance was 29,530, with approximately 2,000 Leeds fans.

After an early chance for Forest, we found ourselves a goal down within five minutes. Once again our passing let us down; we passed back with not enough pace on the ball, giving them the chance to nip in and score. It meant we had to come back from behind again after giving the opposition a goal lead. On 15 minutes, though, Forest should have been a man down. Harrison beat their man and was bearing down on goal with only the goalie to beat when he was brought down. As the last man, their player should have walked but instead the ref only gave him a yellow card. Once again the interpretation of rules by the officials shows a complete difference of opinion when they deal with our players and the opposition. Make no mistake about it, but if that had been the other way around our player would have walked. We hadn't given up and came close from a corner when Alioski's header was kicked off the line. Just before the break we went down to ten men when the referee showed Phillips a straight red after a late tackle. I'd be biased if I said he could have been shown a yellow for it, but their player rolled and rolled around which I think swayed the referee. I agree he was late with the tackle, but when I see decisions never go our way in similar situations and with the earlier last-man tackle only given a yellow, the officials seem to make rules to suit themselves. Just after that we could have been two-goals down when another bad pass was intercepted, but luckily for us Peacock-Farrell made a great save to deny them.

At half-time there were lots of discussions going on, and as we queued for the ladies this young girl said we were s**t! It gave us a laugh in the sense that she didn't beat about the bush when saying what she thought. At the time, though, we were still in with a chance as we were only a goal down. I went down to the front and my flag had been knocked down. Apparently once all the kids saw the players they were trying to get to them so I could hardly blame them.

Clarke came on again at the start of the second half in place of Harrison (he had looked to be playing better and maybe that is something he needs, a run in the team). Although we were down to ten men, it was Leeds who took the game to Forest as we showed the best form of defence is attack. Hernandez brought a save out of their keeper before Clarke pulled a goal back when he hit his shot from the edge of the area to equalise. I was chuffed to bits for the lad, but again he didn't really get a chance to celebrate as we got on with the game. We took the lead after Jansson headed the ball back across the goal for Alioski to smash the ball into the net. Apparently it was Berardi who led the way with a mini pitch invasion to celebrate with the team! After coming from behind it would have been good to see the game out, but with at least 25 minutes remaining it wasn't to be. As the Leeds fans started singing we are top of the league and asking Karanka to stay I thought noooo … don't sing that as it's the kiss of death! With Forest getting the run of the ball once again, they equalised within five minutes as the songs came to bite us on the bum. Clarke came close once again before we let the game slip from our grasp when we failed to clear a corner and they scored their third. If we thought we were home and dry after our second goal, we were mistaken

as we'd stopped attacking and let them get back into the game. They scored a fourth on the break, although someone mentioned it was offside, but it wouldn't have made any difference to the final score though. We did try to get back into the game but sadly being down to ten men showed in the end, which was a shame. We stay top of the league despite the defeat. It was nice seeing a couple of our young fans getting Jansson and Ayling's shirts.

Next week sees the start of the FA Cup with our visit on Sunday to QPR for a 2pm kick-off to link in with overseas fans viewing. I have no problem it being viewed that way but why on earth it couldn't have stayed as a Saturday kick-off is beyond me. My friend Carole wants us to go out straight away as we have a small squad and can't afford to have a cup run. My stance is that the FA Cup should be taken seriously and I don't want the towel thrown in like the last two years at Sutton and Newport. We'll know soon enough which way it will go so see you there.

QPR (A), FA CUP THIRD ROUND – 6 JANUARY 2019

With a 5am wake up call, I for one was looking forward to this FA Cup tie. Winning breeds winning as far as I'm concerned and I certainly don't want the capitulation that occurred after our third-round defeats in the last two years. Time will tell now what happens next, but at this moment in time I am going to watch Leeds United play and want them to win.

Regarding the furore surrounding the Stoke away tickets and many regular fans not getting them, my stance is that after away season tickets have been handed out, they need a small allocation of tickets for those fans who have only missed one or two games who do not have an away season ticket. As the club know which fans do not miss any games and stay with them through thick and thin, good times and bad, loyalty should be rewarded in my opinion. All this talk of these loyal fans being super fans, thinking they are entitled to tickets and having a closed shop, is wrong. These fans have built up their long-term loyalty over the years and should be looked after before the free for all. As for the talk of entitlement, I have no problem with anyone wanting to apply for tickets given the chance, but with the accusations towards those who have earned their loyalty over the years, the same can be said of those fans saying they are entitled to one too as they don't get a chance to build their loyalty up. When things weren't going so well on the pitch last season, there were unsold tickets, so there was a chance. That is no different to what these loyal fans are being accused of. All I am saying is there are a small number of fans who should be looked after too. This created a topic of conversation at our pub stop in Uxbridge prior to the game.

Bielsa had already named his squad for today's game and said he was taking the game seriously, which was a breath of fresh air. I never ever want to go to a game where the towel has been thrown in prior to it as that is a disgrace to the travelling support. If we go out fair and square that's a different matter. I thought we'd arrived very early for the game but it only dawned on me when it was announced over the tannoy that it was 15 minutes to kick-off that it was a 2pm start for overseas broadcasting. As usual I'd forgotten, as well as thinking we'd be home at 2am by forgetting it was an afternoon kick-off and not an evening one. I blame it on the early start lol.

The team: Peacock-Farrell, Ayling, Harrison, Shackleton, Halme, Davis, Forshaw, Baker, Roberts, Clarke and Alioski. Subs: Pearce for Halme (46), Kun Temenuzhkov (making his debut aged 18) for Pearce (79) and Clarke Oduor (making his debut aged 19) for Davis (87). Leeds lost the game 2-1, with Halme scoring the Leeds goal (25). Attendance was 11,637, with 3,148 Leeds fans.

The game kicked off with our team having an average age of 22, and those on the bench an average age of 19. The kids put up a good fight today and the future looks bright. We were unlucky not to take the lead within a minute of the start with Roberts's shot hitting the inside of both posts then bouncing out. With loads of Leeds fans still coming into the ground at that point, what a start that would have been, but sadly it wasn't to be. Unfortunately QPR took the lead when they were awarded a penalty. I wasn't surprised to see it awarded but I'm sure if it had been at the other end it wouldn't have been given. Within three minutes we were level, with a hard free kick from Baker initially saved by their keeper and the rebound put in from young Halme. Although QPR looked dangerous on the break, Peacock-Farrell kept them out with some good saves. I thought we got on top towards the end of the first half and Alioski came close a couple of times. His never-say-die attitude caught QPR in possession as he came away with the ball to set up another attack. After one QPR attack when BPF made the save, it was good to see Ayling on the line behind him, but in this instance he wasn't needed. I thought Leeds had been listening to me by having players on the posts.

Sadly that proved not to be the case in the second half as we were beaten by another set piece from QPR, but if someone had been on the back post helping, this could have been prevented in my opinion. That is one thing I am very surprised not to see being implemented by Leeds as it is an obvious flaw from my point of view, especially as I was brought up seeing the best in Bremner and Reaney putting that into practice. The number of goals they saved being scored by kicking the ball off the line was invaluable. We also missed Halme's height in the second half as he was subbed at half-time, apparently because he'd already been booked. I'm not sure if it was his booking as it looked like someone had a word in the ref's ear, who then proceeded to book Halme for a foul. Tom Pearce was brought on in his first game since injury but found he was also subbed later in the game. Peacock-Farrell continued to make saves to keep QPR out and we ourselves had a couple of good chances to score, and I thought we still had a good chance up to that point. Once they scored from the set piece and we changed our formation, although we kept trying, I thought we were off the boil by then. Baker put a couple of hard passes to our wing which were good, but on the whole I was disappointed in his whole performance, especially in the first half. He still has to up his game a lot more for me, but I think it was important that both he and Harrison played a full 90 minutes. One lad going out behind me at the end of the game shouted it was a long way to come to see shit. I wouldn't go that far as I thought we played some good football and I thought our youngsters did really well when called upon. As we walked back to the coaches my daughter Dani and I were

keeping a watchful eye on the police horses up ahead as the sounds of things starting to kick-off appeared around us. As the police were speaking to some QPR fans, a couple of Leeds fans had another one square up to them, as a police horse came to break it up. I've no idea what happened in the first place as I don't even think the Leeds fans were singing at that time.

Those fans who wanted us to go out of the FA Cup so we can concentrate on the league have now got their wish. I'd be very happy to admit that was a good thing in the long run but only time will tell. The one good thing is we didn't roll over and die and put up some fight today, which can only be a positive. As we play Derby at home this coming Friday, this is a must-win game for us.

DERBY COUNTY (H) – 11 JANUARY 2019

When you are feeling down, the best therapy you can get is head to watch your football team. What an evening at Elland Road, with the best performance of the season and a team playing for each other. After #spygate erupted on social media today, with Derby accusing a person of acting suspiciously outside their training ground of being a Leeds spy, I just laughed. I remember standing outside a fence watching the famous Leeds United team train on Fullerton Park before it became all prima donna like. I'd be happy to see that become the norm again and I can't see what all the fuss is about. Leeds fans, as usual, took the mickey and Legsy in the Peacock had brought his binoculars to the game. Whilst in there it showed on the TV that Bielsa said he was the guilty party as it was a common thing in Argentina to spy on the opposition. All I will say is there is nothing to feel guilty about and Lampard needs to grow up! With a great sing song before we headed into the ground – our spirits were certainly high. In a conversation last week I'd said I wasn't worried about tonight at all. I'd asked my granddaughter Hannah why she hadn't brought her scarf with her as she'd come with my daughter Danielle and we'd met near the ground. With that we found out that some girls on stilts were handing out free scarves to those kids without one, which was really good to see, so Hannah must have known.

The team: Peacock-Farrell, Cooper (back from injury), Jansson, Alioski, Harrison, Clarke (making his first start), Hernandez (back from injury), Forshaw, Klich, Roofe and Ayling. Subs: Shackleton for Harrison (63) and Davis for Clarke (79). Leeds won the game 2-0, with goals from Roofe (20) and Harrison (47). Attendance was 34,668, with 1,238 Derby fans.

There was a cracking atmosphere as the teams came out and it looked like #spygate was not having the effect that Lampard wanted as the whole Leeds United club came together as one. We kicked off and went straight on the attack and the ref pointed to the spot as Alioski was brought down in the first minute, only for the linesman to put his flag up for offside. As I've defended Alioski in the past, it isn't always him who's offside; the officials don't seem to know what offside is, especially when someone said the TV replay had shown him onside! The ref then changed his mind and from then on it looked like someone had given him a flea in his ear for daring to give Leeds United anything. The number of fouls, late and dirty, that Derby made on our players only

for the ref to either play on or not give us anything from them just had me shaking my head. As we've seen so many times, our players do not get the same treatment because instead of a yellow we get shown a straight red. Derby were very lucky to still have 11 players on at the end of the game that's for sure. Leeds carried on with an electrifying pace and Forshaw was all over the place, as was Alioski. They weren't the only ones, though, because everyone was fighting for the ball in packs and helping each other out as we put Derby under constant pressure. With a fantastic WACCOE around the ground and scarves waving everywhere – it looked and sounded an absolutely wondrous sight and it was certainly moving. The sound of the singing, too, was out of this world as Leeds fans became the 12th man. Jack Clarke once again proved his worth as he provided the pass that Roofe got on the end to stick into the net to send Leeds fans into raptures. After having the penalty given then not given, this was justice for us! Leeds were playing some fantastic football and battling for everything and some of the footwork was mesmerising. Obviously Derby couldn't get the better of us so resorted to bad fouls instead. They had their first shot well wide just after the half-hour mark and managed to put us under pressure in the last minutes of the first half. The first half, though, had belonged to Leeds and I can't remember the last time I've seen such a one-sided game for a long time. It was so good to see, though, and we still looked to have plenty in us as our fitness levels show how far we have come since Bielsa joined us.

As I was talking to my friends downstairs at half-time, I said we'll have to go up as Leeds are going to score straight away. As we were behind the betting stand I asked this man to let me through as Leeds were going to score straight away and I needed to get back up into the stand. He said if we did he'd come and find me and asked me where I stood, so I said on the Kop! He said I'd had a senior moment as we laughed at what I'd said. I told the ones at the end of our row what I'd said as the game kicked off. What more can I say, but I was dead right wasn't I? Within two minutes Clarke did some great attacking to the left of us as he got past their player and Alioski passed it back for Harrison to put the ball into the net to give us a two-goal lead! I put my arms in the air shouting I knew it as Leeds fans celebrated everywhere. What a start to the second half! We carried on where we had left off as we continued to put Derby under pressure. I wasn't worried for most of the game as we just swarmed around Derby every time they got the ball. We came close a few times but weren't able to add to the goal tally, but we'd still played really well. I only got nervous at the end as Derby had a couple of attacks and I didn't want them to get anything out of the game. The game ended as Jansson ran rings around Derby, who did the only thing they could do by bringing him down with a bad foul. That should have been a sending off in my eyes, but of course it was only a yellow. As Pontus limped off the pitch at the end he looked to be in a lot of pain. As Clarke was getting interviewed at the end of the game for man of the match, Klich was taking the mickey by pretending he'd got some binoculars! Gallows humour is the Leeds United way.

I'm actually glad we've played tonight now as a relaxing weekend is ahead of us and we can watch the other results at leisure. Our performance tonight will have made others sit up and take notice. We head to Stoke next week and I don't think we should be scared of anyone. Just keep doing what we are doing Leeds and take each game as it comes.

STOKE CITY (A) – 19 JANUARY 2019

It was so sad to hear that Toby Nye, our little Leeds fan, had lost his battle with Neuroblastoma last weekend. As soon as I heard the news the tears were streaming down my face as I felt the pain his family will be suffering having lost a child too. It was great to see the tribute before the game, with Evie, who goes on our coach, and a Stoke fan holding up a City shirt with Toby's surname on the back. He also got a rousing send off on six minutes from the whole stadium which was very moving. RIP Toby and my thoughts are with his family.

Well Leeds United, and in particular Marcelo Bielsa, have hit the headlines well and truly this week after #spygate watching Derby County train. What a mountain out of a molehill and sour grapes from Lampard, what a whinger. After seeing the FA and EFL were going to investigate this, Bielsa showed his integrity and honesty by giving the whole world a 90-minute PowerPoint presentation on Derby. He knows more about Derby than Lampard ever would and you know something, he'd found all that out long before the training-ground incident. The bloke found was even on public land and didn't do anything wrong. I love Bielsa more and more and he so reminds me of Don Revie. He loved his dossiers too and if Bielsa can emulate Revie in any way, which I do believe he can, we are in good hands going into the future. Don't ever change Marcelo Bielsa

because you are a breath of fresh air, especially after all the corruption that has been going on in the game for years and the prima donnas should take a leaf out of your book. They may even learn something! I went on a first aid training course this week and as usual was wearing my Leeds things. I would like to thank Des for buying *The Sleeping Giant Awakens, Leeds United 2016-17* and *Back to Reality, Leeds United 2017-18* (a big thank you to my friend Sue for getting the latter one too). I would also like to thank Andy for buying *Follow Me and Leeds United* for Harry. I look forward to receiving feedback from all of them. Des had already bought the first three books I've written and it was great to get the feedback that he enjoyed reading them all. The funny thing on the course was being asked if anyone wanted to be a trouble maker whilst someone else was performing CPR; well I had to volunteer didn't I? I can be a pest, never stop talking and also can definitely relate to it despite never wanting any trouble near me. I have to say all the others on the course wanted me to be shut up lol! They've never had anyone quite like it I think and I couldn't stop chuckling to myself afterwards.

As we headed to Stoke I couldn't believe that there were still loads of media outlets and failed pundits sticking their oar in about #spygate. With false accusations still being peddled left, right and centre, plus references for us to be docked three points, it is about time they all grew up! Leeds have done nothing wrong and if teams don't want anyone to watch them play, don't do it in public but behind closed doors!

I fell asleep on the way to Stoke and opened my eyes to see all the fields covered in snow and not much visibility, so I was glad I was on a coach. Luckily our snow at home had melted by the time I left to go to Leeds. After a stop in Leek we arrived at the ground, only for me to realise that it was a new ground for me after all. Having visited the Victoria ground numerous times, I'd forgotten they'd moved. Their old ground hadn't been a happy hunting ground for us many times football wise, especially losing our 29-game unbeaten run there on 23 February 1974. Our fans had a laugh despite losing 6-2 and 7-2 two seasons running. And I recall getting ambushed at the graveyard when going back to the station and our fans singing *Daily Express* to me, Sue, Carole and Linda on 13 September 1975 when our photo appeared in the paper. This iconic photo taken outside the West Stand showing the facade is the front cover of my first book *Follow Me and Leeds United*. Is there any wonder I hate red!

The team: Peacock-Farrell, Ayling, Clarke, Jansson, Cooper, Klich, Forshaw, Roofe, Hernandez, Harrison and Alioski. Subs: Roberts for Harrison (61) and Jordan Stevens for Klich (76). Leeds lost the game 2-1, with Alioski getting our consolation goal (90+5). Attendance was 28,586, with 2,919 Leeds fans.

As soon as the game kicked off we got covered in beer courtesy of a Stoke fan at the other side of the divide; was there really any need for that? It didn't take long to realise we were up against it from both the officials and Stoke. In the first few minutes their player dived as if he had been shot right in front of the linesman, who, instead of being reprimanded, was awarded a free kick. I could

see that Stoke wouldn't be a pushover, though, as they looked very strong. They had just replaced their manager so teams normally up their game for that reason, but also when they play us too. We were still able to move the ball around well as we tried to build an attack, and sometimes we were very successful in tight spaces, but not all the time. There weren't many clear chances for us but we came close a couple of times. When Stoke were awarded a free kick outside the area, Peacock-Farrell was lining his wall up. When he crouched down to get a good look, I wondered if he had received some pointers when warming up before the game from our keeper Kiko Casilla, signed from Real Madrid this week. He made a great save tipping the ball over the crossbar and also made another good save to deny Stoke. I still had high hopes at half-time, as we went in level, that we could get something out of the game.

As I took my glasses off at half-time, one of the lenses fell out so I couldn't wear them for the second half, but I hoped all the play would be coming towards us with Leeds attacking. Unfortunately, within five minutes of the second half starting, Stoke took the lead. We had cleared the ball only for it to be headed back into the area by one of our players, which resulted in Stoke getting the ball into the net. That was a shame because it meant we were up against it once more. We did have a chance to get back into the game when Hernandez was fouled just outside the box, but the referee just ignored it. I couldn't believe it, especially as Stoke nearly got a goal from the breakaway. Even I saw the blatant handball from their player, which got a deserved booking. As Stoke broke away they looked to be through on goal, only for Jansson to make a great tackle at

167

the last minute to deny them a scoring chance. The game took a bizarre and unwelcome turn as Jansson was chasing back and went down as the Stoke man shook him off and Peacock-Farrell made a great save to deny them a second goal. The referee once again showed his true colours with a terrible decision, sending Jansson off not before giving Stoke a free kick outside the area! A disgraceful decision, despite the referee trying to indicate that somehow as he fell Jansson handled the ball. As Pontus was being escorted off the pitch, he took his shirt off and headed to the Leeds fans but had to shrug the stewards off in doing so. He gave his shirt away and looked to be having all sorts of issues with the stewards, and I'm sure I saw someone manhandle him in the tunnel.

Just 15 minutes from the end, not long after Jansson received his marching orders, I decided I'd make my way over to the left of the stand to get my flag. I managed to get across two sections and then had to force my way down the steps, where there was no space to do it due to all the fans standing on them. After a battle I made it to the bottom, and we were unlucky not to score when Ayling's header was saved by their keeper. Stoke then got a second goal to put the game beyond our reach, despite Alioski getting a goal back at the death. If it wasn't for us being reduced to ten men I think we would have got a draw at least. I took a photo of a very happy little boy with Pontus's shirt, and thank you for making the effort for him to get it. As we were starting to leave the stand some Leeds fans got very agitated with a Leeds steward accusing him of obstructing Pontus. I wasn't sure what it was all about at that time when someone asked me what was happening. Despite the loss, we remain at the top of the Championship. Let's hope we get back to winning ways next week at Rotherham.

ROTHERHAM (A) – 26 JANUARY 2019

Yesterday saw the sad day of little Toby Nye being laid to rest, but not before Leeds fans lined up outside the East Stand to give him a fantastic send off. Sleep tight little man and my thoughts are with all your family and friends.

On a personal note, this last week is one I hope my family never has to go through again. My stress levels were already through the roof at work when the news we dreaded happening was confirmed. This all ended badly yesterday when my youngest daughter sadly lost her dog. When my children hurt, I hurt, so a sh*t week got even sh**ter. I need my Leeds United family to get me through the bad times and reduce my stress! I should remember this is Leeds United I am talking about, but seriously this is my get away from it all to keep me going.

We left the Peacock at 12.45pm for the short trip to Rotherham, with me sleeping all the way there. As we headed to the turnstiles it was nice to see Phil Thumbsup Cresswell back again after his recent illness and catch up with a chat. Thanks should also go to those people I spoke to before the game as their support is invaluable. I'd heard we weren't allowed our flags up today for some reason but thought I would still check it out. Apparently because it was a full house there was nowhere to put them! I beg to differ with the full house, as there were plenty of empty red seats

around the ground. Last season we had hung them in front of the top disabled area with no issues, so why couldn't they go there again? What a ridiculous decision, from my point of view, because what harm do they do and they show how far and wide our support is?

The team: Today saw the debut of our goalie from Real Madrid, Kiko Casilla, Ayling, Cooper, Phillips, Alioski, Klich, Roofe, Hernandez, Clarke, Harrison and Forshaw. Subs: Roberts for Clarke (45), Shackleton for Harrison (88) and Davis for Hernandez (90 + 6). Leeds won the game 2-1, with Klich scoring both our goals (51 and 86) after we went a goal down in the 25th minute. Attendance was 11,259, with 2,317 Leeds fans.

As the game kicked off Leeds had a lot of possession, but it seemed like we were trying to walk the ball into the net and not really getting any clear chances to score. Rotherham didn't look to be too much of a threat for a long period, then they suddenly upped their game. As I was telling Leeds to step up a gear too, Rotherham let fly with a long-range strike that beat Casilla into the top corner to put them into the lead. It was that dé ja vue moment once again as the first half died a death from our point of view as it looked like history could be repeating itself. Despite a couple of attacks, our best moment came with a shot from Harrison bringing out a good save from their keeper to leave us a goal down at half-time. My stomach started to churn with that familiar feeling of things going wrong.

A few of us ladies had a chat at half-time about the game and then I said, 'Right, we need a positive mental attitude and Leeds are going to win.' Another one said yes we are going to win 3-1! Well the score may have been wrong but we did the trick so well done girls!

With the second half underway, it became clear that if we put pressure on Rotherham they would get nervy and wilt. Within six minutes we were level when Rotherham failed to clear the ball, handballed it in the process, but Klich was able to poke the ball home from close range. It seemed an age before it went over the line, but Leeds got straight on with the game as the fans celebrated. Their keeper pulled off a couple of saves before Casilla made a great save to deny Rotherham a second goal. We started to put some pressure on Rotherham's goal and you could see their players starting to panic. As they started time wasting I said I hoped we could make them pay for that and get the winner. After some great play from Harrison on the left in front of us, the ball came across to Klich in the middle, who struck a great shot into the corner of the goal to send the Leeds fans wild. Klich is scoring goals was sung again and again and as I love the singing and chanting this is just what I needed, plus the win and three points of course. To say only four minutes added time was on the board, the game kept going for nearly three minutes more, which sadly saw Phillips booked as he took one for the team and Hernandez go off with a possible injury.

As we headed out of the ground into the rain, which had apparently been falling during the second half too, Leeds stayed top of the league. This was one of those games that we had to win, and although there is still a long way to go, Leeds, just keep getting the points please.

Next week sees the late kick-off against Norwich who are one of 11 clubs who have written a letter to the EFL demanding an investigation into Leeds and #spygate. All I can say is they need to grow up because Leeds did nothing wrong. If you train in public and anyone watching is on public property, then my answer to those 11 clubs is tough! I want to get to the game in good time as I am meeting one of the Nottingham Whites who managed to order my book *Back to Reality, Leeds United 2017-18* from WH Smith. He wants me to sign it for him so will look forward to meeting him to do just that.

CHAPTER 8

NORWICH CITY (H) – 2 FEBRUARY 2019

As usual things are never straight forward for Leeds United. Although lots of fans stayed up for the transfer deadline on Thursday evening, with the imminent signing of Dan James from Swansea, I went to bed. It was only the next day that I found out the deal was off due to Swansea in-fighting, but I found the way they'd handled it was deplorable. What a terrible thing to do to a young player who was sat at his 'new' club waiting for things to be finalised. Having just got home from the game tonight and hearing Swansea have parted ways with their chairman, it looks like they have lots going on behind the scenes. I really liked Swansea at one time due to them playing in white and the supporters having a say in the running of the club. How things change!

My granddaughter Laura and I bumped into some Irish lads from Enniskillen as we headed to The Peacock. The pub itself was absolutely heaving before the game, and I didn't even attempt to get to the bar, which was about five deep everywhere. There was a good atmosphere though, with plenty of singing. I met Mick from the Nottingham Whites who had bought one of my books to sign. He then bought *Follow Me and Leeds United* from me too so I hope he enjoys the read. He gave me some fantastic feedback from reading my book *Back to Reality, Leeds United 2017-18* and I thank him for that. I'd already bumped into Matt prior to getting to the Peacock, and thanks to him and also Linsey and Katie for buying this book also. As always I appreciate the support.

Fans had laid flowers at Billy's statue in memory of Toby Nye and there was also a minute's applause at the start of the game for both Toby and a little girl, Sophie, a Norwich City fan, who had also died from cancer, as well as ex-Leeds player Phil Masinga. Life can be very cruel, sadly.

The team: Casilla, Cooper, Jansson, Ayling, Harrison, Alioski, Roofe, Hernandez, Roberts, Forshaw and Klich. Subs: Douglas for Harrison (46), Clarke for Hernandez, (46) and Bamford for Roberts (63). Leeds lost the game 3-1, with Bamford scoring for Leeds (90+1). Attendance was 36,524, with 2,465 Norwich fans.

The ground was rocking as the game kicked off with a sell-out, which included a full away end for once. The scarves held up all around the ground looked spectacular and I loved seeing that again. Leeds started off on the attack but within five minutes of the start were once again having to come from behind as Norwich took the lead. We gave away a free kick on the edge of the box and the ball found the top corner of the net in front of us via a deflection off the wall. We had a good chance to equalise as the ball fell to Alioski in the box, but his shot skimmed across the front of the goal going wide. We had a couple of shots on target which were easily saved by their keeper. The referee should have twice booked two of the Norwich players for diving and cheating once the game stopped, but he didn't even speak to them. With Norwich being one of the teams to send a letter regarding our #spygate to the EFL, they had also painted the away dressing room

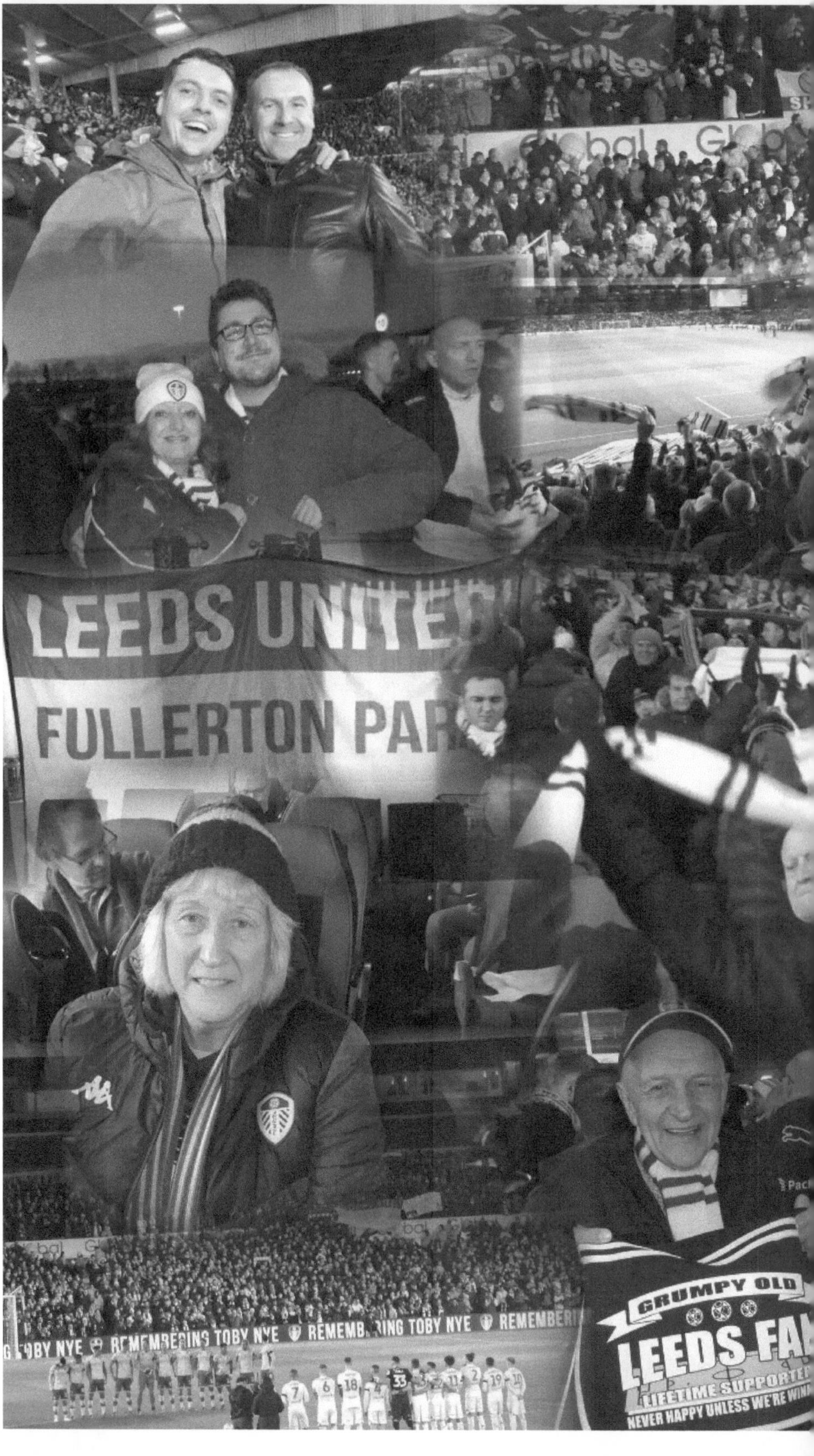
LEEDS
FULLERTON
REMEMBERING TOBY NYE
GRUMPY OLD
LEEDS

pink to try and gain an advantage – it just shows what double standards they have. Before half-time we had a great chance with Roberts through on goal, only for him to be brought down by their keeper. I thought he was out of his area so it wouldn't be a penalty, but as he was the last man he should have walked. A booking only sufficed but our resulting free kick was poor. Norwich were looking stronger than us as we looked weak when trying to get the ball from them. Even when we won the ball back we would give it away easily. Forshaw looked very calm as he took the ball then suddenly lost it. The ball just ran perfectly for Norwich as their player tapped it into the net after an initial strike deflected into his path to put them two goals up. Before the game I'd been asked if I was worried about playing Norwich and I said no. I only concentrate on Leeds United and take no notice of other teams. I will always make my judgements when watching the game myself. I realised we had a mountain to climb but thought we had a few players not pulling their weight. We had a different formation today with both Roberts and Roofe playing, but I felt it wasn't working well at all. Once again Harrison looked lightweight and he hasn't proved to me that he deserves a place in the starting line-up, only as an impact sub probably. Roofe was being well shackled and to be honest I think we missed Phillips in the team. Bielsa made his judgement to keep him on the bench today, but I think it was a mistake not to have him on the pitch. Ayling also looks to be struggling and is definitely not playing well. That said, we got the ball into the net just on the half-time whistle and it took me a minute to realise the ref had disallowed it. Their keeper lost the ball and it should have stood. Sorry I forgot we are not allowed to challenge in the penalty area!

We were still positive going into the second half, even though we were two goals down. Both Harrison and Hernandez were subbed for Douglas and Clarke, but it didn't make a difference to the way we played. I thought Douglas was very poor when he came on and would much rather have put Alioski at left-back and brought Phillips on. It was ages before we got the ball to Clarke too, but when he did get it he always looked dangerous. Norwich were still the stronger of the teams overall, but their play acting I can well do without, although we were still giving the ball away far too easily. Maybe when things are so difficult getting near the penalty area we should try having more shots from outside the box. I know many will go skyward but catching the keeper unawares may work. To cap it all, Norwich got a third goal when the ball went through Casilla's legs to put the score beyond doubt. Bamford hit the crossbar before getting a consolation goal for us in injury time. With the home terraces emptying at great speed, we stayed where we were until the bitter end. It was a very disappointing game for Leeds and I don't think we played well at all, only in small patches.

As always, we have to move on and that will be for the Boro game next week which is now another early kick-off, apparently on police advice. I will take the game as it comes even though it will be tough. There is still a long way to go to see how the season ends, but anyone can beat anyone in this division as we found out today.

MIDDLESBROUGH (A) – 9 FEBRUARY 2019

First of all, I want to wish a speedy recovery to young Jack Clarke and hope that he is okay after an incident in the dugout in the second half resulted in him being taken to hospital. This resulted in 12 minutes of injury time, which also included time added on for subs and time wasting by Boro.

The #spygate saga rose its head again yesterday, with the EFL saying they needed more time to go over their observations. I hope this means that Lampard will be brought to task for exaggerating what happened and look into the cheating of other teams etc. I also realise that pigs may fly too! It's a disgrace and they aren't fit for purpose as we didn't do anything wrong. What isn't even questionable either is they don't even try to hide their biased treatment against Leeds United anymore which shows how blatant it is.

I have made sure I have passed on my opinions about home and away tickets to Leeds United, the Leeds United Supporters' Trust (LUST) and the Leeds United Supporters' Club. I have also completed a survey for LUST and suggest if you are a member and feel strongly about this that you ensure you share those opinions. There is a forthcoming meeting with the club, as far as I'm aware, to discuss these findings.

With the LFU AGM coming up, I am hoping to attend this on a personal level and as a representative of a group of fans. I know there has been a lot of differing opinions being floated around regarding some people wanting their money back, which is their right. Personally, mine will stay in for whatever project is coming next.

As we headed to Boro on a really windy and stormy day, it reminded me of last year when we had bad snow that prevented lots of our fans getting to it. By the time we got to Leeds and on our way to our stop in Green Hammerton, the rain had stopped and the sun was shining. The wind was always going to have an impact on the game, though. The time we had at the club passed really quickly as there was plenty of chatting, laughs and support given amongst us and before we knew it we were on our way to the police escort. By the time we got there it had left the services so, with another three coaches, we set off for the ground in convoy without an escort. Unfortunately, due to traffic, taking a wrong turn and eventually getting into the car park late, we only got in the ground two minutes before kick-off. At least we made it, but the teams were already on the pitch as I headed to the end to hang my flag up next to the Shropshire Whites flag.

The team: Casilla, Ayling, Cooper, Jansson, Phillips, Alioski, Harrison, Bamford, Roofe, Clarke and Klich. Subs: Hernandez for Clarke (46), Roberts for Klich (58) and Shackleton for Ayling (80). Score was 1-1, with Phillips scoring for Leeds (90+11) to equalise at the death. Attendance was 30,881, with approximately 4,500 Leeds fans.

Today was always going to be an important game to try and get us back on track after last week's defeat by Norwich. Bielsa doesn't make many changes, and although I would have liked to see Shackleton start in place of Ayling he stuck with the latter. Ayling has been struggling for me

and maybe a stint on the bench would fully benefit his recovery from his recent injury. One thing I will not condone, though, is people tweeting abuse at him; he is a member of our team and doesn't deserve that regardless of whether he plays well or not. That goes for any of our players. We had a couple of early chances but didn't get any on target. One thing that didn't make sense was us putting high balls in, which, under the conditions and Boro having height in their defence, didn't work. We need to play to our strengths with the ball being on the floor. We had Casilla to thank for making a great save to deny Boro the lead. On 22 minutes Leeds fans joined in with clapping as a tribute to a Boro fan who was killed recently. I got really angry with Leeds a couple of times as we were on the attack, but instead of going forwards we passed it back to Casilla, which put us under pressure and gave Boro the impetus to attack. They were needless decisions, especially when they nearly scored. Our best form of defence is attack, which has been proven time after time. Boro came close with a corner as their player headed it over – luckily for us, as it looked like Casilla took his eyes off the ball as their player got to the ball first.

At the start of the second half Hernandez came on in place of Clarke. Within two minutes our change of tactics contributed to Boro taking the lead as their player ended up in loads of space at the edge of the box. As the ball hit the back of the net that sinking feeling in my stomach appeared again. Despite Boro taking the lead, we tried taking the game to them and weren't giving up. We didn't always get a run of the ball sadly, but we were still trying to get into the game. We came close a couple of times and we should have taken our chance when Bamford hit the ball wide from close range when it really should have hit the back of the net. Their keeper was leading a charmed life when he made a couple of point-blank saves to keep us out. As Boro started play acting and time wasting, this wound up the Leeds fans. As their player took ages to get off the pitch, the referee wasn't even watching him as he stopped, clapped the Boro fans and hugged his players before eventually getting off the pitch. A couple of minutes after Shackleton came on in place of Ayling, Leeds won a corner. Instead of us taking it, everything halted and I couldn't understand why until someone said something had happened in the Leeds dug out. I saw the paramedics there as I zoomed in with my camera but couldn't see who it was. The game stopped for a long while so I went to get my flag; the game resumed as our player was put on a stretcher. It was only afterwards that I found out it was Clarke who needed treatment and was taken to hospital after being taken ill. Fingers crossed it isn't anything too serious and he makes a full and quick recovery. I'd said to one of the Shropshire lads that we needed to play until the final whistle on 90 minutes then realised that it was already past that. I then said until 102 minutes instead and never give up.

As the game resumed, I decided to wait on the stairs in the corner of the stand. I did think that if Leeds scored it wouldn't be a good place to be as the fans would come hurtling down the stairs. Well I must have had a premonition as we did indeed get that equaliser on 101 minutes. As the ball flew across the area it was headed in to the net by Phillips. I couldn't work out who had the final touch of the ball until Leeds fans started singing 'He's magic you know, Phillips the Yorkshire Perlo'. I was right in the thick of it as fans came flying down the stairs to the front all going nuts. I moved to the side, grabbed my bag as my feet shot out from under me as I'd no grip on them. Luckily as I fell my bum landed on the seat so I was fine, but it could have been so much worse. I then stood on my seat to see and take photos as Leeds fans celebrated. I did see a little lad being lifted over the front and taken by our stewards down the tunnel. I hope he was okay and not sure if he'd just been separated from whoever was with him by the celebrations. As we celebrated as if it was a winner, that goal meant we won a very hard point, which could prove to be a turning point for us. The conditions were not brilliant today, but we persevered, which got us a just result. That goal was for Jack Clarke!

My camera suffered a fault as it wouldn't let me see the screen at the back of it but worked okay on a selfie. I think I've sorted it but as we have Swansea at home next Wednesday it is needed! With QPR away being changed due to their progress in the FA Cup, it means even more changes to our forthcoming fixtures on top of the live TV games. Let's get Swansea over the line first so see you there.

SWANSEA (H) – 13 FEBRUARY 2019

It was good to hear that Jack Clarke was released from hospital, and although he is still having more tests this week I wish him a speedy recovery and look forward to seeing him back on the pitch.

Personally, my days of multi-tasking and trying to be superwoman came to an abrupt end yesterday as the soap opera my family seems to have has taken its toll on me. Things will happen

that we've to deal with and although it has its challenges, it means I've had to take a step back. Thanks to the fans who helped me tonight, and, despite my tears, I am grateful for their time and support which is appreciated.

Elland Road had another sold-out sign tonight showing tremendous support from Leeds fans, with the only empty seats being in the away end. As I waited for my sister Erica to meet me at Billy's statue, it was nice to chat to a number of fans and take their photos. My granddaughter Hannah and daughter Danielle both went into the ground early, whilst I had a quick visit to the Peacock before going into the ground. As the teams came out there was a great atmosphere around the stands. Everyone stood as one to give a minute's applause to Gordon Banks who was in goal when England won the World Cup in 1966, who has died.

The team: Casilla, Jansson (celebrating his 28th birthday today), Ayling (making his 100th appearance for the club), Cooper, Hernandez, Klich, Roofe, Bamford, Alioski, Harrison and Phillips. Subs: Roberts for Bamford (71), Shackleton for Klich (77) and Davis for Hernandez (90+1). Leeds won the game 2-1, with goals by Jansson (20) and Harrison (34). Attendance was 34,044, with approximately 400 Swansea fans.

The game started off with Leeds seeing plenty of the ball and having a couple of shots off target. As the game went on we looked to settle down more and we took the lead in the 20th minute after a corner. The ball came back in to the box and Jansson put the ball into the net in front of the South Stand, which saw great celebrations all around the ground. Even though Swansea kept running at us and always looked dangerous, Leeds were always still looking to attack. Today it looked like all the players had upped their game, which was good to see. There were always going to be some passes that went astray, but everyone was fighting to get the ball, with players backing each other up. Swansea came close to scoring with a free kick before Leeds went further in front with a goal from Harrison to give us some breathing space. The lad next to me was giving an update regarding Preston taking a two-goal lead against Norwich, who themselves had missed a penalty. As I'd said to someone before the game, we need to concentrate on us as anyone can beat anyone in this division. We came close to a third goal before the break but went in at half-time in the lead.

Swansea came out for the second half looking to get back into the game and for me they never gave up and always looked dangerous. We were still seeing plenty of the ball, attacking and playing some really good football but couldn't get that third goal despite coming close. We should have got a penalty when Bamford was wrestled to the ground but none was given, surprise, surprise. Casilla was called upon to make a couple of important saves but was sent the wrong way when Swansea were awarded a penalty in the final minutes of the half. I said that was not a good place to give away a free kick and the lad in front of me turned around and said it's a penalty! Despite Swansea being given a lifeline, Leeds battled and the crowd were still urging them on until the final whistle blew. What a relief to realise we'd got the points and gone back to the top of the league as Norwich lost their game at Preston.

Due to QPR being changed, it means we have a free Saturday this week, which is a shame. The one thing it will do before our next game against Bolton at Elland Road on 23 February is give our players time to get over any injuries. I would much rather play games on a Saturday than midweek though. I can't say anyone played badly tonight and they all played as a team which was good to see.

BOLTON WANDERERS (H) – 23 FEBRUARY 2019

Firstly, it was good to hear that Jack Clarke's recent illness has been diagnosed as a virus and that he is back in light training. Get better soon Jack and I look forward to seeing you back on the pitch.

The soap opera of Leeds United reflects my own family, with always something going on. This time it was the news that we had been found guilty of #spygate by the EFL and had been fined £200,000. What a load of rubbish, as this ended up out of hand due to lies that were spread. What I want to know is why Frank Lampard has not been brought up for bringing the game into disrepute for spreading those lies? That isn't showing goodwill towards us so what is different? The answer is nothing, it's just that we are called Leeds United and there is one rule for us and one for everyone else. No one will change my mind about that as I've seen too much of it sadly, and although the club accepted the fine to move on quickly, I would have liked to have seen us fight back for once.

Today was a glorious spring day as we headed to Elland Road for an actual Saturday 3pm kick-off and another sell-out crowd from the home fans. It certainly makes you feel better and blows the clouds away when the weather is nice like this. As we'd gone down to third on goal difference

due to the postponement of our game against QPR, my stance is that we should ignore everyone else and concentrate on Leeds United only. Just keep getting the points and see where the land lies later on.

It was nice to meet up with some Dublin Whites by Billy's statue and also in the Peacock and I appreciate the comments made to me. Some Ajax fans were in the Peacock too, who had come to watch Leeds, and I met a group from Malaysia who had come to Elland Road for the first time as well. Such is the pull of Leeds United; this shows our worldwide support including our Scandinavian contingent who had travelled to the game as well. I'd agreed to meet up with the Nottingham Whites for a photo by Don Revie's statue before heading into the ground. My granddaughter Laura went in the family stand today with my sister Erica and niece Siobhan and she was looking forward to sitting down! It's standing room only in the Kop so my granddaughter Alexis, who is smaller, took on that role today, with some help from my daughter Danielle.

The team: Casilla, Ayling, Cooper, Jansson, Klich, Phillips, Bamford, Harrison, Alioski, Roberts and Hernandez. Subs: Dallas for Roberts (81) and Shackleton for Ayling (90+4). Attendance was 34,144, with approximately 500 Bolton fans. Leeds won the game 2-1, with a penalty by Bamford (16) and Alioski (68) with the winner.

There was a good atmosphere around the ground as the game kicked off. It was Bolton who came close to scoring in the first few minutes, with Casilla making the save before Alioski came close with a shot that was tipped over the bar. As is usual, Bolton were showing that they were going to raise their game as they were playing us. Also, with some of the tackles flying in, they were going to play by foul means if they had to. They got away with a yellow card for a couple even though the ref pulled them up for it. As we attacked the South Stand, Roberts was brought down for a blatant penalty which was given straight away by the ref. That is only our second one of the season and after a few arguments as to who would be our penalty taker, Bamford stepped up to send the keeper the wrong way to put us into the lead on 16 minutes. As soon as he'd given that decision for us, it seemed that the ref had realised he couldn't do anything in our favour as every little touch for a while was given as a free kick for Bolton. Casilla had my heart in my mouth a few times as he raced off his line to clear the ball, with one coming very close to one of the Bolton players.

As it was, Bolton got an equaliser ten minutes later when we couldn't clear the ball. Harrison did well to head the ball off the line with Casilla beaten, but then we didn't clear it and after another three attempts, with the ball running kindly for Bolton, they put the ball into the net. They weren't going to give up easily that's for sure. They could have taken the lead not long after this, but luckily the ball went wide of the post. We had a couple of great chances and Bamford's header didn't have enough pace on it and was saved by their keeper, which was a shame as it was a good move. Their goalkeeper denied us with a great save too, so with the scores evens we went into the break.

186

With the second half underway, some great play saw Ayling get the ball in the penalty area, who was unlucky not to score as the ball went past the wrong side of the post. Casilla was called into action again, saving a long-range shot. As Leeds looked to bring Dallas on as sub, he was suddenly sent to run up and down the line again as Bielsa decided to leave things as they were for a while longer. This paid off as Leeds scored again to retake the lead when Alioski's cross dipped and their keeper was unable to save it. I haven't seen it again, but it's been mentioned it was deflected, but as long as it's a goal that's all that counts. A few minutes later, after a bad foul on Alioski, it all kicked off on the touchline and ended up with two of the Bolton players booked and their manager Phil Parkinson sent off. Bielsa walked past the entire melee, went to see that Alioski was okay and was as cool as a cucumber! I think his opposite number should have taken a leaf out of his book! We came close a couple of times but were unable to put some breathing space between the teams, and, despite Bolton coming close in the last minutes of the game, we were able to see it out and claim the three points.

As we ended the first half on the attack, we were awarded a corner but the referee decided to blow the whistle and not let us take it. I've mentioned this because in injury time in the second half we had already played the five minutes plus more and Bolton were awarded a corner. The ref carried on playing until their corner was taken but luckily we headed the ball clear and got the win. With everything the same at the top of the table, we take on QPR next and as usual it won't be easy as they'll raise their game no doubt. Just go out there Leeds United and get the three points as that's all I want!

QPR (A) – 26 FEBRUARY 2019

As Leeds headed to QPR for the rearranged game, I tried to ignore all the stats coming out about their recent bad run of defeats. Having followed Leeds for so long, I know the form books go out of the window when they play us, but for once I was hoping we would have the impetus. I would much rather play games on the said day and get the points rather than have a game in hand. Time would tell how that would pan out. I want to say a big thank you to my friend Sue for being a shoulder to cry on.

The team: Casilla, Ayling, Cooper, Jansson, Bamford, Hernandez, Phillips, Alioski, Roberts, Klich and Harrison. Subs: Douglas for Phillips (65), Dallas for Ayling (73) and Brown for Alioski (81). Leeds lost the game 1-0. Attendance was 14,763, with 3,105 Leeds fans.

Leeds came out on the attack but the final ball was wide. Their goalie made a great save to deny us a goal from Phillip's header from another attack. The closest we came to scoring was when the ball went across the penalty area and when it looked like Bamford was going to score; unfortunately, he missed connecting with it. I wasn't sure if he'd taken his eyes off the ball or whether it was just too far in front of him, as it was hard to say at the time. The saying that you have to take your chances when they are there comes to mind. QPR had been time wasting from the off but were continuing to frustrate Leeds by always trying to get the ball back off us. Roberts kept winning the ball but then lost it or gave it away and there were a lot of show-boating flicks from a few players that didn't come to anything as QPR won it back. Despite us not scoring, the Leeds fans in the stand had been fantastic, with constant singing and creating a great atmosphere. This always lifts the mood for me as I love the singing. Leeds continued to have a lot of possession but were constantly passing the ball back to Casilla. He made one great save to keep out QPR and another one when he put his head on the line, so to speak. We do seem to be passing the ball back a lot at the moment though and should remember the best form of defence is attack. Liam Cooper went off with a head injury that needed stitching just before half-time. You could see Leeds just wanted to contain QPR to ensure they didn't score until he came back on the pitch just before the whistle blew.

At half-time I was talking to some fans who said it had been rubbish so far. I didn't think it had been too bad as we'd been attacking, but got that familiar sinking feeling in my stomach. QPR took the lead in the first few minutes of the second half, which came from us not keeping possession. Our passing hadn't been crisp, it was short, and QPR took advantage to fight for the ball, putting our players under pressure. As we lost the ball in the far right-hand corner from us, the ball flew across the penalty area and their man was behind our players to put the ball into the net from close range. I'd no idea where Casilla was at this stage and will need to see what happened. The mistake of losing the ball at the back had cost us dearly. QPR went on the attack and Casilla was forced into making a couple of good saves to keep them out. Alioski brought out a great save from their keeper as he crossed the ball from the left when it looked ready to dip under the bar. When Phillips was subbed I was mystified because there were plenty of other players I would have brought off before him. I had

to hope that Bielsa knew what he was doing. Douglas had a fantastic chance to score, only to blast the ball high into the stand. It should have been on target at least. Frustrations were creeping in amongst the support with the miss, although the fans were still getting behind the team. We had another great chance to equalise, but the ball wouldn't go in after first Dallas, then Bamford had their goalkeeper making the saves and living a charmed life. I felt if we could get one goal then we'd get another, but the longer the game went on the more I knew it wasn't going to happen. Izzy Brown came on for his debut; many Leeds fans think he is going to make a difference to us. My first impressions of him weren't great, because his first tackle could have had him seeing red as soon as he got on the pitch. I would have taken a draw but the loss saw Leeds stay in third place on goal difference. Scoring is an issue at the moment, that's for sure, despite all the possession we are having.

Knowing how demoralised I felt at the end of the game, I could empathise with Bielsa after seeing the photo of him on social media slumped on his haunches. We have to 'Keep Fighting' every game and still get as many points as possible as it is not over yet. Please don't put us through the horrors of the play-offs Leeds, we need to aspire to automatic promotion and it isn't over until the fat lady sings, so they say! Keep the faith Leeds fans, as always we will have our ups and downs as we keep Marching on Together! For those fans who had to endure the normalities of motorway closures on an away day, it meant some of our northern contingent didn't get home until 4am; I hope the players appreciate what our supporters do to follow their team. West Bromwich Albion at home is going to be another key game this week so see you there.

CHAPTER 9

WEST BROMWICH ALBION (H) – 1 MARCH 2019

Before the game I couldn't have told you what day we were on, never mind who we were playing, plus I'd forgotten the game had been moved for Sky. Suffering from extreme lethargy, I needed a pick me up that's for sure. The Navan Whites were bringing their new flag with them and I'd arranged to meet them for a photo. We also had a 'spy' in the camp today as Jeff Astle's daughter had travelled with some Leeds fans to the game. For anyone who doesn't know, Astle scored a goal in 1971 at Elland Road when referee Ray Tinkler let them play on with a player in an offside position. Tinkler has never been forgiven for that decision by Leeds fans, which cost us the league. It also resulted in us having to play our first four games of the next season away from home, two at Huddersfield, one at Hull and one at Hillsborough, due to a few fans running on the pitch in protest.

There was a fantastic atmosphere in the Peacock before the game and lots of singing, which was great. I'm not sure if Dave Aalbers had got in there prior to kick-off. I'd spoken to him the day before about Leeds United for a story that will be published on the Dutch site VICE Sports. He couldn't have chosen a better game to come to either.

The team: Casilla, Jansson, Cooper, Phillips, Hernandez, Harrison, Roberts, Bamford, Alioski and Ayling. Subs: Dallas for Harrison (77) and Shackleton for Roberts (90+2). Leeds won the game 4-0, with goals from Hernandez (20 seconds), Bamford (28 and 63) and Alioski (90+2). Attendance was 35,808 with approximately 2,500 WBA fans (they'd had official transport put on for them to attend the game today which forced them to stay until the end of the game!) It was also another sold-out game.

I'd just made my way to my row and was on my way to my seat when I stopped in my tracks. Our first attack of the game had seen us go straight to the opposite end and I thought we're going to score! As the ball hit the back of the net from Hernandez, Elland Road erupted as I tried to keep my beret on my head and take photos amongst the celebrating fans. What a start that was. In my last blog I'd said that Leeds have to remember that the best form of defence is attack, so I'm pleased that Bielsa had taken my advice lol! As the crescendo of noise erupted around Elland Road with an electrifying atmosphere, we couldn't have asked for a better start. Leeds were fighting for every ball and it was great to see. That raised the tempo of the game even more as Leeds drove forward in search of more goals. As is the norm at Elland Road, the ref was giving free kicks galore to West Brom as every little tap saw them go down, whereas we didn't get the same benefit. Admittedly some were free kicks but others were questionable, especially when he let things go against us. That did not deter Leeds, though, as Bamford was put through by Roberts to score a second goal for us, ramping up the atmosphere even more. The celebrating Leeds fans couldn't believe what they were seeing after the recent defeat at QPR; what a contrast as each player was fighting for each other and playing as a team. It was a fantastic sight to see and the only game that came close in my point of view was the Derby home game. West Brom did come close to scoring as their long-range shot tested Casilla, who was off his line. Luckily for us he tipped the ball over the crossbar, making a great save. To be honest, though, we limited West Brom to rare chances, such was our domination of the game. We had further chances before half-time but it was great to go into the break with a two-goal lead.

The one thing I did notice, though, which Peacock-Farrell got loads of stick for, was Casilla's positioning in goal from free kicks outside the area. For example, when the free kick was taken in front of the Kop, the wall was lined up to the right and he stood to the left of that, leaving a massive gap at the other side of the goal. West Brom only had to lift the ball over the wall for a clear chance, as there was no way Casilla would have got to the ball and would have needed a man on the line. The only thing I will say on that score is that, to me, it obviously isn't down to the player but the way they are trained that makes them leave the big gap.

It was great having a half-time chat after the first half we'd just seen as everyone was in good spirits. I said I needed to get back to my seat just in case we did a repeat of the first half by scoring immediately. I did have to wait a little bit for that to happen though. Admittedly I did get a little nervous at the start of the second half as that was when West Brom were at their most dangerous. You can always tell when I get nervous as the lad in front of me said I had started swearing, oops! It didn't take Leeds long to get back into the game though, closing them down and fighting for everything. Roberts was having his best game of the season for me, although I'd forgotten he'd come from West Brom as it was so long ago, plus Bamford then scored his second goal of the game to put us three goals up. Fantastic scenes all around the ground as the crowd never stopped with their support and singing. I loved every minute of that and it is the best therapy I could ask for. We had even more chances but their goalie made the saves to keep us out. When Shackleton came on during injury time, one of the first things he did was run down the wing to the left of us and cross the ball. When this happened a second time the crowd erupted as the ball hit the back of the net. I thought he'd scored, but it turned out Alioski was in the middle to put it in the back of the net and give us a convincing win at 4-0 to put us back to the top of the table. Happy, happy Leeds fans, players and staff; in fact, everyone connected with us were ecstatic that the game had turned out that way. Prior to the game someone said we would get beaten 2-1. My response was I didn't predict scores and would make my judgement on what I saw on the pitch, but it was a must win game for us. Thank you Leeds United for making my night as I loved it. This is what makes supporting Leeds United special, our fans and the team playing like this. It was lovely to see a photo of Bielsa after this game smiling away but he still wouldn't take any credit, it was always everyone else who should be given the praise. What a humble man and a fantastic ambassador for the game, and it's a shame there are not more people like him. The bonding he has done with the team is fantastic to see, all for one and one for all, I love it!

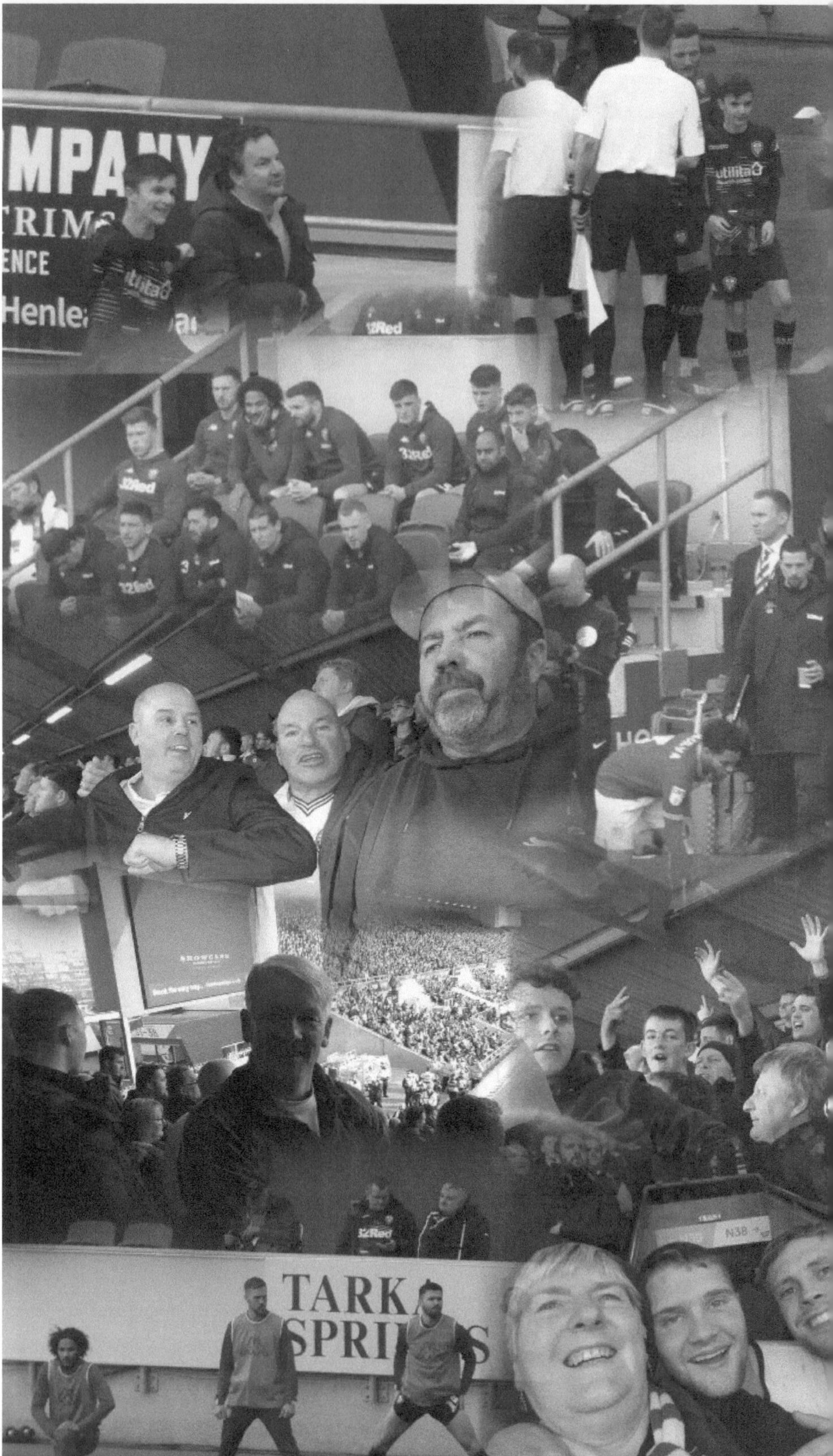
MPANY
TRIMS
ENCE
Henle
32Red
TARKA
SPRI

We have a nice weekend to look forward to now but, as I've said, we should just concentrate on Leeds United and forget about everyone else. We stood up to be counted today and will have sent shivers down the spine of others around us. Keep going Leeds and onto Bristol next week so see you there.

BRISTOL CITY (A) – 9 MARCH 2019

Hearing loads of Leeds fans and neutrals had found their tickets for today's game had been cancelled by Bristol I felt for them. What makes that decision a mockery was seeing half of the away stand seats had been covered over and out of bounds when they could have accommodated these fans. Never mind the money that Bristol threw away, it felt that after the recent #spygate incident when the Bristol chairman was crying out for us to lose points, that this decision was carrying on a vendetta against our club. Well instead of us losing points, can I say thank you Bristol for another three points today, making six in total from you!

Once again, I want to say a big thank you to all those fans for showing their kindness and support after a particularly gruelling week for my family. With my husband three weeks into his treatment fighting cancer, there are so many others going through similar challenges. I'd encourage anyone to talk about these things as it does help. Today is my therapy and the recharging of my batteries to help me get through this, so I was able to catch up on my sleep both going and coming back from the game. Also I appreciate the comments from those who love reading my blog and for those wanting their photos taken.

We arrived at the ground in plenty of time for kick-off so my daughter Danielle and I headed to the front of the stand to put my flag up in a prime position near the corner flag. Finding my seat in the stand was very difficult as each section had the same numbered seats, which caused confusion. As one fan said someone was in his seat, I intervened and said to check which section he was in. The steward thanked me for my explanation with this. When I eventually found what I thought was my seat, there was no one there who normally stands near me so who knows if it was the right one? I stayed there for the first half though.

The team: Casilla, Ayling, Cooper, Jansson, Alioski, Harrison, Bamford, Hernandez, Phillips, Roberts and Klich. Subs: Dallas for Bamford (57), Douglas for Harrison (75) and Berardi for Klich (83). Attendance was 24,832, with 2,680 Leeds fans at the game and another 2,000 at the beam back at Elland Road. Leeds won 1-0, with Bamford scoring for Leeds (9), which pleased my friend Sue as she won the golden goal on the coach!

The atmosphere was brilliant and the Leeds fans were in full voice, which is something I love. Singing is another thing that is very therapeutic! As the game kicked off there were a few slips on the field so I began to wonder if the rumours about the pitch getting an extra watering were true. It didn't take us long to get to grips with it though, so I assumed it was just a rumour. Bristol had the first chance before Leeds took the lead early on in the ninth minute. Alioski put a fantastic ball over to the right-hand side, which Ayling headed into the path of Bamford, who put the ball into the net. Cue, there was beer thrown everywhere amongst the celebrating Leeds fans. One lad had already fallen over the back of our seats and ended up on the floor next to me. As I looked for the players celebrating too, I realised when I couldn't see them that someone was down in the penalty area and saw on the replay that Bamford had collided with the post on scoring. Luckily, he was able to carry on after treatment. I thought he'd hit his head but later reports on a knee injury may mean I was wrong. He did go down again later on at the same time as Phillips who had to put the ball out as he needed treatment too.

As Bristol tried to get an attack going, they started making mistakes, with the ball going out of play on numerous occasions. We came close again when Roberts brought a save out of their keeper. Leeds looked very comfortable on the ball and to me Bristol only threatened from set pieces. Luckily we dealt with most of them comfortably, although a couple of times Casilla raced off his line and we were lucky to not be punished for it. The only time Bristol looked like scoring was when we messed about with the ball on the right-hand side just before the break. Alioski was in acres of space on the left-hand side but we insisted on playing the ball on the right. This put us into trouble as Bristol won the ball, but luck was on our side for once and we kept them out. Ten minutes before the break, though, the Bristol fans in the stand to our left were streaming downstairs so obviously they weren't impressed with the way their team were playing.

At half-time I went downstairs and when trying to find the ladies was pointed in one direction. I saw all the lads going through that door so thought it can't be that way. Well I was wrong, but whoever designed the ladies and gents next door to each other wants a kick up the bum! All that does is make the lads use our loos instead of sticking to their own! It would help if they shut the door whilst in a cubicle too, not that they cared!

After taking loads of photos when I got back under the stand, I tried finding Tina, who I was meeting as she wanted to buy my first book *Follow Me and Leeds United*. Thank you for the support it is appreciated. We were both at the opposite ends of the stand but then made things worse by both trying to find each other so it was vice versa. I headed to the middle of the stand behind the goal and at least Tina found me there! Someone else is wanting some of my books, having bought one last week, but neither of us could remember which one he had so I will have to look at my photos to find out.

Bristol came out fighting more in the second half, but we still managed to get to grips with them as we continued to look for a second goal. Some fantastic work by Harrison just in front of us saw him beat three men before passing the ball to Roberts, whose shot was saved easily by their keeper. It's a shame it didn't have any power in it. With another set piece Casilla looked way off his line, but despite that we were able to keep Bristol out. When Casilla made a save, all of a sudden there was an outcry, with their fans screaming off, off. It was only afterwards I saw a replay of what happened and it looked like their player caught Casilla. They put heads together but then as the ref approached the Bristol player stepped back before throwing his head back as if he had been shot. Anyway, for once the ref saw someone trying to cheat and get someone sent off or booked, but it could have been worse. Suddenly the Bristol fans woke up, but they'd been very poor, whereas the Leeds fans were getting behind the team and it really was great. As a player was down injured, Tina and I went down underneath the stand to get to where my flag was as there was no way we were going to be able to get through the crowd standing in the gangway. As I've no grips on my boots, we had to tread gingerly as the floors were wet through and it looked like the beer throwers had been having a field day!

I hadn't seen the blue flare that was set off when we scored as it was right at the other end of the stand. It was only when I was talking to one of our stewards at the end of the game that he said someone suffered greatly from breathing in the smoke and came down to the front where he was promptly sick. A couple of the Bristol stewards were very impressed with my flag too, and when asked who my hero was, well there is only one and that is Billy Bremner!

As 90 minutes appeared on the clock, six minutes of injury time was put up. I got nervous a couple of times, but on the whole Leeds continued to battle and keep them out so I wasn't too bad, although I was counting down the minutes. When the ref blew for time the Leeds fans celebrated and sang their hearts out as the team came round for a deserved round of applause. Jansson was roaring to the fans and no one went to leave immediately as the Leeds fans savoured the moment.

Another three points put us back into second spot after both Norwich and Sheffield United had won, respectively, last night and this dinner time.

As we came out of the ground a lad from Russia, who had come with some friends I know to the game, came to say hello so I got some photos. Our coach was on the same street so we didn't have far to walk. We didn't gain much time on the other coaches and by the time we got around the roundabout the rest were just being escorted away from the ground, so we joined them. We stopped at the services to change drivers and a coach with fans in red and white were getting off theirs at the same time. As we were coming out of the loos, this woman looked at my scarf as I asked who they were: Sunderland was the answer, who had been to Wycombe Wanderers. It was only at this point I realised they weren't in our division because as usual I'd forgotten they'd been relegated. The smallest person in their team had been fighting and, as Danielle checked on the scores, there had been sending offs very late in the game which had finished very late. At least the meeting with opposition fans at the services was more civilised, although that was definitely not the case during the 70s!

Another win gets us closer to our dream, so keep going and onto Reading next. Don't worry about anyone else, only us, and keep getting the points please.

READING (A) – 12 MARCH 2019

After a bad night and an early morning call to Jimmy's Leeds, I was looking forward to catching up on my sleep on the journey to Reading. Again, thank you to fans who spoke to me in support of my husband and me as it is greatly appreciated. I'd seen Andy Loftus post that the plaque for Chris and Kev has been cleaned and restored by Richard Illingworth. As the anniversary of their murders in Turkey nears, I want to say well done as he has done a brilliant job. I was glad I wasn't driving to the game with the rain and wind causing problems, but things had calmed down by the time we got to the ground just before kick-off.

Reports from those who attended the under-23s game at Elland Road on Monday gave some fantastic feedback. They were playing the same way as the first team and there are some more great prospects coming through, which is good to hear. Seeing it all falling into place behind the scenes is certainly good news for our club and long may it continue. The other good news was hearing Jack Clarke had returned to the under-23s after his recent illness, so that is a relief knowing he is okay.

The team: Casilla, Jansson, Cooper, Ayling, Alioski, Roberts, Bamford, Harrison, Hernandez, Phillips and Klich. Subs: Dallas for Ayling (57), Shackleton for Roberts (69) and Douglas for Klich (74). Leeds won the game 3-0, with Klich (14) and Hernandez scoring two (22 and 43). Attendance was 17,701, with 2,071 Leeds fans.

We started off with a lot of possession but seemed nervy, causing misplaced passes that Reading took advantage of, but Casilla made the save to keep them out. Once our nerves settled, though, we took the game by the scruff of the neck. Ayling ran down the right, passed the ball into

the middle for Klich to score after Bamford had dummied the ball to put us into an early lead. 'Klich is scoring goals' rang out from the Leeds fans, who were in good voice. We'd sold out again, although we were only given just over 2,000 tickets due to Reading having a 'singing area' in the same stand as us. I'd commented that I hoped we could score plenty of goals to shut that drum up! We took the game to Reading then and took a further lead when Ayling once again passed the ball in and Hernandez hit his shot off the foot of the post which went into the goal. The Leeds fans celebrated in style as that would hopefully take the pressure off us. We hadn't stopped there as we continued on the attack, coming close from Klich before Bamford brought a save out of their goalie. Just before half-time we scored a third when Hernandez hit a fantastic strike after Bamford released the ball to him. We had taken to scoring from distance today instead of walking the ball into the net, which had taken Reading by surprise! 3-0 at half-time saw some really happy Leeds fans going into the break.

Again, at half-time we saw lads who couldn't be bothered to find their own loos and were using the ladies! We did manage to shoo some lads out of there and told them to find their own! The Leeds fans below the stand were having a great sing song, although two decided to climb up onto the overhead pipes, which had my heart in my mouth. I can't understand those who throw their beer around though, especially when it costs so much, plus I had to walk gingerly to make sure I didn't fall on the wet floor!

The second half saw Leeds take their feet off the pedal as we started playing further back. Unfortunately that saw the nerves kick in a bit for me as that's what normally catches us out. We did still attack, but this format saw Reading get into the game more. When Ayling tried getting out of the way of a Reading player, their fans were screaming at him to be sent off. There was no way he could get out of the way and the ref spoke to him. As he'd already been booked, Leeds did the right thing and subbed him as he was in danger of being sent to the dressing room. He'd played well though. As the game continued my nerves eased a bit as I saw Leeds were coping well with everything thrown at them. We came so close to a fourth goal when Bamford should have done better, and then Hernandez saw his shot go inches wide. Bamford came close again, which saw the Reading fans start to give him some stick, so the Leeds fans upped their support of him! Hernandez was very unlucky not to get his hat-trick, though, when the goalie made a save initially and he was unable to get to the rebound. Leeds managed to keep another clean sheet as we took the three points to go back to the top of the league and sent a great Leeds support home happy. As Reading hasn't been a happy hunting ground for us it was great to get the win too.

For once we didn't have to negotiate closed motorways on the way home and had a relatively good journey, although the wind closer to Yorkshire and on the M62 was still causing issues.

Saturday sees a crunch game with Sheffield United coming to Elland Road for the early kick-off. With another sell-out home crowd, both teams have a good run behind them. We know what we have to do Leeds – three points please.

SHEFFIELD UNITED (H) – 16 MARCH 2019

The weather was foul as my granddaughter Hannah and I headed to Elland Road, and this storm showed no signs of abating. With flooded roads to contend with on the way home, I'll be glad when the weather improves. At least we didn't have snow like Northumberland and Scotland, though. For once it wasn't just the home crowd that was sold out as Sheff Utd had sold all their tickets too, so we were looking at a full house. I'd seen on Facebook that a couple had arrived from Malaysia for their honeymoon on what would be their first visit to Elland Road. Unfortunately, I didn't manage to catch up with them for a photo but hope they had a good day. I was also meeting Mark in the Peacock, which I'd assumed was to take his photo. It turned out that I was to take part in an interview for the documentary *100 years of Leeds United*, which was a surprise, but of course I did that. I heard someone shout something about two magpies when they passed me outside the South Stand. Prior to Mark arriving I was talking to some lads, one of whom had read my books and said he had enjoyed them. Thanks for the feedback it is appreciated.

Hannah wanted to go into the ground early so I made sure she got through the turnstiles before going and renewing our season tickets. Now the paper copies had come through I was able to renew them as the auto cup scheme can be chosen, whereas online you don't get that option. I have sent the suggestion to the club for the auto cup scheme to be added to the online renewal because it would make it easier and I know I'm not the only one who waits for the paper copy to arrive for that reason.

The team: Casilla, Ayling, Cooper, Jansson, Harrison, Phillips, Klich, Bamford, Roberts, Alioski and Hernandez. Subs: Douglas for Harrison (57), Clarke for Klich (77) and Dallas for Ayling (77). Leeds lost the game 1-0 and had Casilla sent off in the second half. Attendance was 37,004, with 2,641 Sheff Utd fans.

As the game kicked off there was a minute's applause for Bill Fotherby who died this week. He was chairman of Leeds during our promotion from the Second Division and winning the title in the First Division, which saw Leeds as the *Last True Champions*.

Leeds started off on the attack before getting a further opportunity a few minutes later when Bamford's shot was blocked. It looked like he tried to place the ball rather than hit it hard, which may have resulted in a better chance. We had another great chance with Harrison but, unlucky for us, he volleyed the ball over. We kept the pressure up and it was a case of hoping we didn't rue the missed chances as we were unable to put the ball into the net. We had limited Sheff Utd to a few attacks, but then just before the break we were passing the ball across the back but we didn't seem to know how to take it forward. With that Sheff Utd got the impetus and nearly made us pay as they were unlucky not to score in the final minutes as they upped their attack. They should have been pulled up with a hand ball for one of them and offside for another but got away with both of those decisions. I was glad for the half time whistle to blow but felt by messing about at the back we had given Sheff Utd some hope. At times we had not taken the swirling wind into consideration, although Alioski managed one great pass across the pitch.

At the start of the second half as we were attacking towards the Kop, I couldn't help but notice their players were built like brick 's**thouses', or so the saying goes. It felt a bit like men against the boys (us) when I compared the players as they were hard to fight off at times. We did have a great chance to take the lead when a fantastic attack saw Klich get to the byline to cross to Roberts, only for his shot to come back off the post. That was probably our best chance of the game but that started my stomach churning as that familiar feeling that we weren't going to score came over me. Unfortunately, it did come back to bite us as Sheff Utd took the lead when Sharp got the better of Cooper before he passed it to his player to score. That said, we did keep on trying and were attacking when Sharp elbowed Jansson, who went down like a ton of bricks. Sadly for us, that slowed the game right down and we lost our momentum. Sheff Utd were closing us down quickly, though, which didn't help. Clarke came on in a double substitution with Dallas. He got to the byline and passed the ball across the goal only for Jansson, who at this time was playing up front, to hit the ball past the post. Leeds were still going in search of an equaliser, which I'd have happily accepted at this late stage, only to be caught out on the counter attack. This time Phillips was overcome and, as Sharp ran past him, Casilla, who was way out of his area, came out and brought him down and was given a straight red card! Down to ten men but there were still a few

minutes left plus injury time, so Jansson had to go in goal. We survived the free kick and in the last minute, when we were awarded a corner, Jansson came out of goal to join the attack, but to no avail as Sheff Utd got the win.

Unfortunately, this defeat means we drop out of the automatic-promotion places, with Sheff Utd jumping into the space. As I've said many times, anyone can beat anyone in this division, but both Sheff Utd and Norwich seem to be living charmed lives at the moment. It isn't over by any means and we still have to go out and get as many points as we can. From shooting on sight at Reading, we reverted to type by trying to walk the ball into the net or taking that one step too many instead of catching their keeper unawares. We could also have taken advantage of the wind behind us, but sadly it wasn't to be. We now have a week off before Millwall at home with the LUDO dinner and dance on the same evening. I tried getting extra tickets for the Millwall game but was unsuccessful once again. Every time I chose tickets and tried to buy them it wouldn't let me. Also, even though sections were showing limited tickets they were all greyed out! You never know there may be the odd ones that come available before the game!

MILLWALL (H) – 30 MARCH 2019

It's not often that a television crew turns up at your house to interview you! I would like to say a big thank you to Mark and the crew for filming me for the *100 years of Leeds United* documentary. I look forward to seeing the finished version of this in due course, which will coincide with the

centenary year of Leeds United being formed. Mark also purchased my book *Follow Me and Leeds United* and later in the day so did Noel from Ireland, so I look forward to receiving feedback in due course.

Next Tuesday I am hoping to attend the funeral of a stalwart Leeds United fan who I met in the 1970s, Trev Horsley, who has sadly died. He was instantly recognisable for wearing a sheepskin coat and was always one of the first people I saw in Leeds station when I travelled to games by train. Next week is a poignant one in many ways for me when the fourth of the month sees the anniversary of my daughter Charlotte's death and also sees the end of cancer treatment for my husband. We've still a long way to go on the latter, especially as he has had a bad week and ended up in hospital. The following day brings the anniversary of the deaths of Christopher Loftus and Kevin Speight, who were murdered in Turkey. My heartfelt thoughts go to all their families on these sad occasions.

We return to Elland Road after the international break to resume our league and promotion challenge. Having slipped back into third after the defeat to Sheff Utd, today is a must win game for us. I've no pre-conception of what will happen but am looking forward to seeing us carry on in the best way we can. Today is a family occasion for us, with my daughter Danielle and I being joined by my three granddaughters Hannah, Laura and Alexis. Two of the girls will be going in the family stand with my sister Erica and one with us in the Kop. It was also nice to catch up with Mark, one of my Selby Whites, when I ran the supporters' club there. After the game, apart from Alexis, we will be going to the Pavilion for the LUDO dinner and dance and will have two excited girls looking forward to meeting the players.

On our way to Leeds I had to pick my granddaughters up in Rastrick then go via Wakefield to pick up Danielle. As I was going a different way, I put the postcode into my satnav, only for me to end up more or less back where I started! I was more bothered about the wasted time in getting to Leeds. We made good time despite that and managed to avoid the long queues by driving via Beeston. At least we managed to meet up with my sister in good time and also David, who'd helped me regarding parking for Preston. We bumped into some of our Norwegian fans and it was the first trip to Elland Road for one of them, who had supported Super Leeds since 1972. I also bumped into some of our fans from Scotland and again it was the first trip in many years for one of them. Thanks for the feedback regarding my blog too, which is appreciated. I'd also been asked to get some photos of the lads with the flags today so needed to be in the ground in good time. I had a quick trip to the Peacock to catch up with friends and it was nice to see some familiar faces.

As I made my way into the ground, there was a happy buzz around with lots of fans enjoying being at the ground with not a Millwall fan in sight. This is what I like about the away fans being in the West Stand and escorted in from the Fullerton Park car park – it means instead of chaos reigning down Elland Road, it is now a calm oasis of our fans. This makes it good for bringing the kids to the game without any antagonisation and I much prefer it that way.

The team: Peacock-Farrell, Ayling, Cooper, Jansson, Klich, Phillips, Hernandez, Roberts, Bamford, Harrison and Alioski. Subs: Douglas for Alioski (45), Clarke for Jansson (67) and Forshaw for Klich (75). Leeds won the game 3-2, with Hernandez getting two (34 and 83) and Ayling getting one (71). Bamford missed a penalty before Hernandez equalised for us, making us do it the hard way. Attendance was 34,910, with 975 Millwall fans.

I'd been asked to move by one of our stewards as I'd moved to the right-hand side of the Kop to get the photos of the kids with flags as they still had the nets up behind the goal. I managed to stay there till just before kick-off, but apparently some fans were complaining as well as it being a legality of not standing on the steps. I made my way to my normal spot, which is something I do every game, for a few more minutes before heading to my seat, which I always do once the game kicks off.

I always base my judgement of the opposition on the pitch as I don't worry about them beforehand. I always say we need to play to our strengths and let the opposition worry about us. It became very clear straight away that Millwall had come to run at us and were a very physical team. Within ten minutes they were ahead when a long ball across the field caught us out before the ball was crossed to the middle for their player to head it into the net. Prior to that, Peacock-Farrell made a good save to keep them out. At times we were at sixes and sevens with their attacks. Coming from behind again was a pain but we didn't let that deter us as we started to see more of the ball and started to attack. When Alioski was brought down in the box and the referee pointed to the spot, I breathed a sigh of relief that we had a chance to get back into the game. Sadly, it was not to be when Bamford's very weak and casual penalty was saved by their keeper. It was a case that we were going to have to do things the hard way. Harrison came close to scoring before we equalised when Ayling passed for Hernandez to put the ball into the net in front of the South Stand, sending the Leeds fans into raptures. Roberts then brought a save out of their keeper with a shot from the edge of the box just before the break.

Leeds started the second half on the attack, having brought Douglas on to replace Alioski. He'd had a couple of hard tackles on him, so I wasn't sure if it was a tactical decision or due to an injury. As Leeds continued to attack we were caught out with a counter attack which saw their player free on the left-hand side of the pitch heading towards the South Stand goal. When it looked like there was only Peacock-Farrell to beat, Cooper came across the box from the right-hand side and fouled the Millwall player who were then awarded a penalty. Sadly, they took the lead from theirs as they sent Peacock-Farrell the wrong way. Although we were behind, the crowd were still getting behind the team as we continued to seek an equaliser. Harrison showed some great footwork in the penalty area as he kept the ball then from Douglas's perfect cross; Ayling, with a brilliant header, put the ball into the net to send everyone wild. Coming back twice from behind to keep the win within our grasp got everyone's hopes up. Leeds weren't stopping there and settling for the draw as everyone raced back to the middle instead of celebrating with the fans; we were going out to win this game, there was no doubt about it. We had now got our tail between our legs and Ayling's goal saw him play like a man possessed as we continued our charge towards the Kop end. We were now attacking with gusto and came close to scoring when their keeper nearly fumbled the ball into the net. Forshaw's great strike from the edge of the box nearly caught him unawares as we won a corner instead. We got the winner after some fantastic work by Tyler Roberts, who stopped the ball from going over the goal line and passed the ball hard across the box where Hernandez was on hand to stick the ball into the net. Cue, wild celebrations around the ground with limbs everywhere and it was hard to keep my feet in the melee. I wouldn't have changed it for the world as the team celebrated with the fans. We'd fought back, never given up and it had paid off. Scenes like this are out of this world and they are what makes being a Leeds United fan special. When the final whistle blew, fans stayed glued to the stands to continue singing and celebrating as Sheff Utd's home fixture against Bristol City had seen them beaten to put us back up into second place. Getting the three points is all that matters to me and I don't care how we do it, but experiencing the winning goal today means I want more of that. We have only seven games left and it is in our hands once again to get that automatic promotion place.

In the second half of the game, I have never wanted to beat someone as much as I did when I found my dislike of Millwall reached fever pitch. With their deliberate goading of the fans in both the Kop and South Stand after scoring their goals, if that isn't inciting trouble I don't know what is? It took until the 81st minute for their goalkeeper to be booked for deliberate time wasting; with every goal kick he went and got a drink before taking the kick. How satisfying it was after our third goal went in as the ground exploded with noise and celebrations. It's funny how he didn't waste any more time after that!

There are some fantastic photos on the official site and also a fantastic vlog from Lewis Deighton when the goal went in. Make sure you have a look as they are well worth seeing. My photos are from a fan for the fans and are a different perspective. I know lots of fans love to have their photos taken but I am aware not everyone does. I was made aware, in no uncertain terms, not to take any photos of one person and share them around, which is their choice and I am happy to adhere to that. I can't remember if I have actually posted a photo or they refused one but either way it isn't a problem. I am always happy to take any photos down that people don't want showing, all that has to be done is to ask nicely.

Next week sees us head to Birmingham for the next stage of our battle for promotion where we come up against Monk once again. With their club having just received a nine-point deduction due to issues with EFL spending rules, they are still outside the relegation places. We want three points regardless Leeds, so let's get them please!

CHAPTER 10

BIRMINGHAM CITY (A) – 6 APRIL 2019

This week has been a very challenging and emotional week. Tuesday saw a great gathering, including lots of Leeds fans, to pay their respects at Trev Horsley's funeral. Thursday was the anniversary of my daughter Charlotte's death and the end of radiotherapy/chemotherapy treatment for my husband Phillip, and yesterday saw the anniversary of the murders of Chris and Kev in Istanbul. I also heard today that Andy Ramshaw, one of my Selby Whites, died this week too and thoughts are with his family and friends. The last couple of days I found a lot of anger in me that sent my stress levels soaring, which culminated in me having a massive meltdown. The one good thing about following Leeds United is the support network from our fans. For those who took time to ask how I was, my husband was, spoke about football, look forward to my blog, follow me on Twitter/Facebook or have bought my books, my heartfelt thanks go to you all. You know who you are and, as always, your support is greatly appreciated.

We had a lot of nervous fans heading to St Andrews today. As it is still too early to build my hopes up, I was just going to wait and make my judgement at the ground. From my point of view

and many others, the only way we can guarantee promotion is to go up automatically. Having been disappointed three times in the play-offs, I don't know many fans who would fancy our chances doing it that way.

The team: Casilla, Ayling, Cooper, Jansson, Harrison, Phillips, Klich, Bamford, Alioski, Roberts and Hernandez. Subs: Dallas for Harrison (45), Roofe for Bamford (70) and Clarke for Klich (70). Leeds lost the game 1-0. Attendance was 24,197, with 2,781 Leeds fans. On the 19th minute, Leeds fans turned their backs to the pitch en masse for a minute in memory of Chris and Kev, as those who were at the game did all those years ago, as it should never have gone ahead after what had happened. It was a game that I'd been too scared to attend so my friend Karen went without me.

I just want to mention the Leeds United mascot, who was brilliant. He came to the Leeds fans doing the salute and was a credit to the club. Leeds came close early on and had plenty of possession but the one thing we couldn't do, was get the ball in the net. The referee showed his credentials early on by missing an elbow on Robert's head plus other pushes but was quick enough to give free kicks the other way for less than he let go with us. The linesman to the left was useless, too, because despite some things happening right in front of him, he ignored them. All this does is give the opposition the impetus. We limited Birmingham to one attack and should have taken the lead when Bamford got to Ayling's cross and the ball looked as if it was going straight into the net. Sadly for us, it hit the post and bounced back into their keeper's arms. To make matters worse,

Birmingham raced to the other end of the pitch in front of the Leeds fans and put the ball into our net to take the lead within a minute of our attack. The case of taking your chances when they are there came back to bite us quickly as we went into the break a goal down.

The second half saw Dallas come on for Harrison and we really should have equalised when he put a cross over to the middle for Bamford to fire over instead of into the net. That was a chance we should have taken. Bamford was really unlucky with his next chance when the keeper made a fantastic save from his header. On another day he could have had a hat-trick! As time went on it looked more and more likely that we weren't going to score, despite the possession we were having, and we had Casilla to thank for making a couple of good saves to keep Birmingham from increasing their lead. Whilst there was only a goal in it we stood a chance of getting back into the game. As it was, Norwich had a convincing win to stay top of the table and Sheff Utd won to leap frog back above us into second place as we slipped down to third. Today had that déjà vu feeling about it; we've been here that many times before and promotion is not going to happen. Although a lot can happen between now and the end of the season, until it is mathematically certain one way or another I won't raise my hopes. The one thing we do still have, though, is a chance so only time will tell what happens.

It was a disappointing game for us today as we weren't really in it collectively as a team. We may have had a lot of possession but unless we are peppering the opposition's goal with shots and putting them under pressure it counts for nothing. With Preston away on Tuesday evening, only a win will do for us. As we are driving to this one, we won't get there until nearer kick-off, so hopefully the traffic will be fine and we will get there on time.

One thing that really disappointed me this week was the club's decision to stop season-ticket holders from being able to buy any tickets for the last game of the season against Aston Villa. Only Gold members were given the opportunity to buy one ticket each. I was going to purchase some in the family stand for my daughters and granddaughters to come to the last game of the season as usual. I stand by my argument on WACCOE that this decision should not have been made for this season but for next, as they changed the goalposts at short notice. As part of the agreement for buying a season ticket at the start of the season, there was priority booking for home games. The club have not looked at the wider picture or the impact that decision has had on fans, who have made plans to attend this game. Having read plenty of posts on social media, it has really hit our overseas fans hard as Norwegians, Hungarian, Dutch, Irish – and even a lady from Argentina – have found that very few of them can now get a ticket for the game, and they make plans well in advance to attend any game at Elland Road, booking flights and accommodation to get the best prices. The decision has also impacted on families where a parent has brought their child all season on their season ticket, but now cannot bring them as they don't have that all-important gold membership. That, to me, is wrong. I can try and get my granddaughter a ticket but there is no way she is going into the family stand on her own! There again, knowing my luck I'd be unsuccessful anyway as I have been unable to buy any extra tickets when they have gone on sale all season. The only way I've managed to get any was when some tickets have come back up for sale. Now that Sky have moved the game to the day after, Sunday, that again has impacted on fans who cannot make the game, sadly.

Part of my personal issues has seen trapped nerves in my back and degeneration of my back and hip. At least I know why I've been getting the pain but they are just more things I could do without in the never-ending story with my family. The saying *things can only get better* couldn't be more apt for us and Leeds United. Don't let us down please – see you at Preston.

PRESTON (A) – 9 APRIL 2019

I was travelling by car to this game as the person who was taking me was in a meeting, so we set off later than we normally would. Because of this, we had a pre-booked parking spot and a big thank you to David Hill for sorting this out for us, it is greatly appreciated. As it was we arrived in plenty of time for kick-off, despite some queuing before joining the M61 and the parking spot being a 15-minute walk from the ground. There were plenty of Leeds fans walking up to the ground at the same time as us, which was unsurprising as we had another away ticket sell-out. A good thing about it was that after the game I was home in Halifax by 11.15pm, which was brilliant!

I went to put my flag up behind the goal and was surprised to see that Preston had made some changes to the layout of the stand since we'd last been there. The first rows of seats were all fenced off so no fans could get to the pitch side. At least I had a prime spot for my flag.

The team: Casilla, Ayling, Cooper, Jansson, Alioski, Hernandez, Bamford, Roberts, Harrison, Klich and Phillips. Subs: Berardi for Harrison (77), Forshaw for Roberts (83) and Roofe for Bamford (90). Leeds won the game 2-0 with a brace for Bamford (62 and 76). Attendance was 18,109, with 5,516 Leeds fans (plus however many were in their ends and the corporate areas).

It was no surprise to see that Bielsa had kept the same team that started at Birmingham. Despite the defeat there, unless there are any injuries he likes to make few changes. Plus I think he also likes to give the players a chance to make amends, especially after a defeat.

Leeds were up to it from the start and looked like a different side to Saturday, despite being the same team. Our first attack brought a save out of their keeper. We continued to attack but, although we came close, we didn't get anything on target. Alioski was down for a while and when I saw him continue with a bandaged head I couldn't remember if he'd had one on when he came out or if that is what had happened to him. The officials were all guilty of ignoring what should have been free kicks to us but giving Preston plenty. When they were pulling Jansson's shirt the linesman to the left was only a few feet away and in full view of him, but he might as well have been on a different planet! More shirt pulling had one fan shouting, 'if you want a Leeds shirt then go and buy your own!' The linesman on the right called an offside, which had everyone around me baffled and screaming that he didn't know what he was doing. Every time Bamford was fouled the ref gave it the other way, saying he was backing in, with one incident late in the game where he was thrown to the ground given to Preston – unbelievable! We didn't have everything our own way, which I always say is down to the free kicks given to the opposition, and Preston always looked like they could score. We had lots of possession again but not many clear-cut chances. The one thing I would like to see again is us peppering the opposition's keeper with shots. My memories of the great Don Revie side are of us hitting the woodwork but also making goalkeepers work by making saves or more importantly letting us score goals. Having shots on target and taking more shots from outside the area would catch keepers unaware, in my opinion.

At half-time I went downstairs where things were getting a little lively. A few women came into the toilets for a smoke as they'd been instructed to do so by the stewards, despite there being no smoking signs everywhere. No one was allowed out of the ground to smoke so some even did that in the concourse. It didn't make sense to me as the gates are opened at half-time at many grounds. Now if it was Ipswich away on the last day of the season I could understand them not wanting to open the doors at half-time as there'd be an invasion of fans without tickets!

As the second half got ready to kick-off, their number four was having a word with the ref. I said he'll be asking him to be nice to Preston. As it was, the same player brought Bamford down when he was clean through and given his marching orders within five minutes of the restart. Phillips came close with the free kick. From then on we kept the pressure on with having an extra man and at this time I felt we could get something from the game. The keeper looked jittery at times, and so he should with thousands of Leeds fans breathing down his neck. With one shot he spilled the ball but recovered enough to catch it at the second attempt. When Bamford's shot was saved by the goalie he looked like he'd a point to prove. Well he certainly did not long after that when he struck a fantastic goal from the edge of the area to send the Leeds fans behind the goal wild. I got hit on the head as the people behind me fell after being pushed from further up the stand. It didn't matter though because Leeds were in front, which was all that mattered. The next thing I saw was Leeds fans being escorted out of the stand to our left with drinks being thrown at them, plus there were loads of Leeds fans in the stand to our right too. We couldn't settle for a one-goal lead and had to go for another. Ayling came close to scoring and hit the post before Bamford got his second of the game with a header as Klich pinpointed the cross in the right place for him to score. I'd written in my blog on Saturday, after the Birmingham game, that on a different day Bamford could have had a hat-trick. I was happy for him to get one today on that basis but, although he came close, we had to settle for two instead.

The win sees us go back into second place as Sheffield Utd play tomorrow at Birmingham. Having seen someone post that we are definitely in the play-offs now, that's fine but I want automatic promotion please. As I kept saying what will be, will be, I was told we don't want to go to Wembley and I quite agree. We have a late kick-off of 5.30pm this coming Saturday with the Sheffield Wednesday game at Elland Road. Having seen some of the Welsh lads after the game who'd said, 'can we do it?' My answer was that I daren't make any predictions as I don't want to jeopardise anything. What we do have is a chance and I would love for us to make things mathematically certain sooner rather than later for that automatic spot. We will know soon enough so see you on Saturday.

SHEFFIELD WEDNESDAY (H) – 13 APRIL 2019

With such a hectic week behind me I'd not really thought about the game today so wasn't unduly worried, and as usual I was going to see what transpired on the pitch. With only five games left and having a later kick-off due to Sky televising today's game, things could change in the table again. As we went through the turnstiles in the Kop, I heard someone say Millwall had a penalty against Sheffield United (who like us are challenging for that automatic spot). I then heard another person say they'd missed the penalty, so we said we'd have to do it the hard way. By the time my daughter Danielle joined us I had no idea that the game had ended in a draw so Sheffield United were only above us on goal difference.

Before the game I'd met Mick Glasby from Nottingham and his friend Alistair, a Glasgow Rangers fan, who had come with him to the game. A big thank you to Mick for buying my second book *Once a Leeds fan, always a Leeds fan*; the support is appreciated and the feedback that he enjoyed reading my first book *Follow Me and Leeds United* was good to hear. As Laura, my

granddaughter, and I got into the ground early we went and stood at the front of the stand to watch the players train before kick-off. There were plenty of fans watching and a young boy next to us was thrilled when he was given one of the t-shirts the players were wearing. Laura wanted to ask Jamie Shackleton for his as she'd had her photo taken with him at the recent LUDO event, but he was at the far side of the ground. One of the Nottingham Whites came up to speak and had a photo taken. Laura decided we needed to go to the other end of the Kop but stopped in the middle behind the goal. As I was speaking to the crew who had come to film me at home for the *100 years of Leeds United* documentary recently, a flying ball caught Laura's arm who was just to the right of me. She was very brave though and said it hadn't hurt, luckily. I showed the crew where our seats were and arranged to go and see them at the end of the game for a chat. As I'd been asked to take photos of one of the mascots, it was also good to be in the ground early for a change.

The team: Casilla, Ayling, Jansson, Berardi, Harrison, Phillips, Klich, Bamford, Roberts, Hernandez and Alioski. Subs: Roofe for Bamford (64), Forshaw for Klich (77) and Dallas for Harrison (86). Leeds won the game 1-0, with a goal by Harrison (65). Attendance was 36,461, with 2,527 Sheffield Wednesday fans.

As the game kicked off it wasn't long before I was confident that Leeds meant business today. Although we'd been turned around so we were attacking the Kop in the first half (it's not often that has happened this season), that didn't deter us. Roberts was very unlucky not to score an early goal, but only because their keeper was playing out of his skin and made a great save. I didn't realise Cooper wasn't playing for a while and that Berardi was on the pitch instead. I knew Ayling was captain but didn't realise why, and it was only afterwards I found out it was because something had happened in the warm up that prevented him starting. Sheffield Wednesday came close when Casilla got beaten when he raced out of goal, but the ball went into the side netting. They had their keeper to thank for saving a header from Harrison, and then Ayling had one kicked off the line when it looked like a certain goal. With the opposition limited in their attacks, they tried time wasting as they were no match for Leeds, but despite all the attacking we went into the break still at 0-0. We had played well though, which was good to see, and had been unlucky not to score.

I went back up in the stand just as the players came out for the restart. We started the second half as we ended the first, on the attack, which was good as I'd said to my friends that we were going to score straight away. Well I didn't get that quite right as it was the 65th minute when we took the lead. I saw the ball crossed in from the right and the next minute everyone was going wild as Elland Road erupted. I had thought the ball had gone straight into the net, but Harrison had, in fact, got on the end of Hernandez's cross to score. We thought we'd managed to score a second goal when Roofe put the ball into the net, only for the linesman to stick his flag up for offside. That was a shame as it would have put the game to bed and there'd have been no comeback for Sheffield Wednesday. Just before time, though, we actually invited them to attack us and I was glad to see the ball hit the side netting. The Leeds crowd had been fantastic and the fans had upped the atmosphere, getting behind the team. When the final whistle blew the scenes around the ground were ones of joy, but also of relief that we had got the win and the three points. There were so many happy fans, which was great to see, and loads shouting hello to me as we made our way outside the disabled entrance to meet the documentary crew. Thanks to all those fans who asked how my husband was, he is now out of hospital with one hurdle behind him and the next one to overcome. The support is appreciated, as always.

I daren't get my hopes up until it is mathematically certain that we can retain second place in the table. I still think Elland Road is the best place to be when we crank up the atmosphere and look forward to seeing us take on Wigan on Good Friday. After seeing how the team fought and played for each other today, it will be good to see them carry on in the same vein. Fingers crossed, we can do this Leeds, keep fighting!

WIGAN (H) –19 APRIL 2019

As I headed to Elland Road with my granddaughter Alexis, the sun was shining, making it a great day for football. On arrival at our parking spot all the stresses from a manic week slipped away because all that mattered was being at the game. Although I've had to limit going on social media recently, I was still aware that we had a lot of fans who were nervous about this game, but I had not really thought about it myself. That said, I saw a lone magpie (damn you), and also the stat of us scoring first and not losing suddenly came into my head (why?), and us being turned around to play facing the Kop made me think that things just may not go our way today. I also found lots of messages appear on my phone that I'd missed over the last few weeks that somehow hadn't shown up until today. I had hoped to bring my husband to the game as I thought it would help his recuperation, but he wasn't well enough to be on the terraces sadly.

We headed to the Peacock as I was meeting Martyn and a colleague from Holland who wanted to do an article for a Dutch magazine, *Staan Tribune*. A few friends joined in with the conversation and it was good to have this opportunity and I look forward to seeing it when it is released in the summer. Whilst meeting my daughter Danielle and niece Sonya at Billy's statue, I took some photos. It was great to get some feedback from one of the Irish lads, who thanked me and said he loved my blogs. I couldn't have a better compliment than being told that what I do is fantastic as it makes him feel like he is there at the games with me. There was also Tom from New York who was attending his first Leeds game. Future stars are two girls who play for the Leeds United Academy. Marta Parodi had arrived in Leeds from Argentina to attend the Villa game. I'm not sure if she'd made the game today or not, but someone had told her to get to the Peacock to enjoy the atmosphere beforehand. Hopefully I'll catch up with her at the Villa game as it would be nice to record her visit with a photo; I wonder if she travelled here with Luciano

Becchio lol? It was also nice to hear during the week that my book *Follow Me and Leeds United* was being read in Costa Rica and that Mark was enjoying the read. His son will also read it after Mark, so it will be interesting to hear a younger generation's view on what it was like following Leeds United during the 70s.

The team: Casilla, Ayling, Jansson, Berardi, Phillips, Klich, Alioski, Hernandez, Harrison, Roberts and Bamford. Subs: Forshaw for Phillips (45), Roofe for Roberts (45) and Clarke for Klich (70). Leeds lost the game 2-1, with Bamford scoring our goal (17). Hernandez's penalty had hit the post a minute earlier, meaning we failed to score from another penalty. It also meant Wigan were reduced to ten men as their player had handled on the line and received a straight red card. Attendance was 34,758, with 743 Wigan fans.

With Sheffield winning their early kick-off game, putting them back into second place, it was vital that we followed suit to go back above them in the table. Leeds were turned around at kick-off for the second home game in a row, which I felt was a shame. It didn't deter us from starting out on the attack, though, and we were unlucky not to get on the scoresheet with our first attack. Wigan looked as if they'd be up for it today as they were a big and strong side. Once their player got sent off and with the penalty miss, I said we'd have to score even more goals then. Within a minute Bamford had indeed scored a great goal to put us into the lead. I was looking forward to us scoring more, despite seeing first a bad back pass, then Casilla being rounded far out from goal, which nearly presented Wigan with an equaliser. We had a couple of shots on target which meant, at that moment, I felt we would be able to score more and Roberts was unlucky not to score when the ball was headed off the line. With another attack, which should have been a corner to us but it wasn't given, Wigan raced to the other end and put the ball into the net to equalise just before the break. This was a bad time for them to score against us and really deflated the Leeds support.

I went back up to my seat before the start of the second half when I suddenly felt very weary. When the team came out it was a surprise to see that both Phillips and Roberts had been subbed by Bielsa. It seemed a strange sub so early on in the game as they both hadn't been playing badly. It also became apparent to me quite quickly that this hadn't worked in the way he'd expected it to. It was more because of the fact that the wrong players had been taken off, in my opinion. What we were up against was a team of very tall, strong players who had built a wall across the back line and were wasting as much time as possible. When they attacked they ran straight through the middle at us and just shook our players off. I felt we were losing the game in midfield because we were attacking high up, but our defence was constantly on the back foot. The worst thing happened when Wigan took the lead as the game already had that déjà vu feel about it. Their keeper made some great saves to keep us out, but we never looked like getting that breakthrough again. We continued to play the same move along the left-hand side, which didn't work and I felt Harrison had a poor game, along with many other players today. I thought he was the one being subbed when Clarke came on, but it was Klich who was taken off instead. Our crossing was poor a lot of the time, but with tall players in the opposition they found it easy to mop them up. Although we did try to take shots many a time, it would have been great for that first-time ball to be hit rather than passing it again to the left as we couldn't make them count. There was lots of tension on the terraces which, along with the team looking the same, meant it didn't bode well for the score line. When the ball went out in front of the West Stand, as Wigan forged another attack, this could have resulted in another goal when the throw-in wasn't given. Luckily for us they didn't, and despite the hope that we could get an equaliser and a point, sadly this didn't materialise as we ended up on the losing side.

With all the Wigan celebrations I didn't realise until we spoke to one of their fans after the game that they'd been in a relegation battle. It wasn't a surprise that once we gave them that lifeline before half-time they'd reacted better than us to get the win. They deserved that win on the day, sadly for us. One thing I must mention that has to stop is those fans who think it is okay to throw things at the opposition players. I know it was frustrating when their player went down in front of the South Stand as it looked like he was play acting, but please, please think about what you are doing. This will go on the referee's report as he went around the penalty area picking all the coins up and handed them to the fourth official. We cannot give the EFL/FA any more opportunities to clamp down on our club as this also happened at a recent game and I haven't heard any outcome of those charges yet. We have had enough battles on our hands to get to where we are and the last things we need are any more to deal with. It matters to me and many others that we take the upper hand, as the Kop did, with the provocation shown to us when Wigan scored their first goal.

With Norwich getting a late equaliser in the late evening kick-off and obviously the Sheffield United win, we are back in third place and out of the automatic-promotion spots. As a support, we all want automatic promotion Leeds, so please do all you can to get those full nine points from the last three games to give us that chance. As today showed, anyone can beat anyone in this division and with Brentford not being a happy hunting ground for us, that is one statistic I would like to change. Over to you Leeds United, please do those of us going to the game proud and change that one!

BRENTFORD (A) – 22 APRIL 2019

After having no nerves up to now, today's game had a different feel to it. Despite sleeping on the way to the services, which I thought would take my mind off things, my stomach churning started with a vengeance. After the Wigan defeat, which was a real downer, it felt like we'd blown our chances of automatic promotion. That has been my choice of guaranteeing promotion for us, as we don't do play-offs, so even though we'd still be in the latter it didn't help my mood. I still sent out a tweet first thing today though saying, 'We can still do it Leeds. Keep fighting until the final whistle

blows.' We've got to have a positive mental attitude despite the nervousness, and I want us to raise the roof as fans for the full 90+ minutes and make the team play out of their skins. The reality, though, was as I feared, we lost the game and, although not mathematically certain at this point, are resigned to the play-offs. With the meltdown underway on social media, what I will say is that it doesn't matter if we'd have taken the play-offs at the start of the season; the reality is that we've blown automatic promotion when it was in our hands. If we'd been in the chasing pack it would have been a fantastic achievement, yes, but we weren't. As usual Leeds United have demoralised their loyal support once more as we've seen it too many times. That said, the season isn't over yet and if by some miracle we do pull this one out of the bag and achieve promotion by the play-offs for once in our lives, I'd be over the moon. All we can do is be there as usual and give them our support like we did at the final whistle today. I'm very downbeat at the moment, but once I've slept on things it never seems as bad. The sad thing is, though, that unless by some miracle we pull it off and win the play-offs, we will have thrown it away, which is hard to take.

It was a beautiful warm and sunny day when we arrived at the ground for the tea-time kick-off, which meant once again that we were playing catch up with those above us having played already. The Leeds crowd were still in a jovial mood ready for us to take the bull by the horns and get a win, despite our poor record at this ground. As we got in the ground, although I was in the seats I went to the front of the standing terrace below to hang my flag at the front.

The team: Casilla, Ayling, Cooper, Jansson, Alioski, Bamford, Roberts, Harrison, Forshaw, Klich and Hernandez. Subs: Dallas for Alioski (12), Roofe for Roberts (58) and Clarke for Jansson (64). Leeds lost the game 2-0, putting them out of the automatic promotion spots, three points behind with an inferior goal difference. Attendance was 11,580, with 1,680 Leeds fans.

From the word go we looked up for it and should have had a cast-iron penalty when Bamford was brought down in the box. As I hadn't put my glasses on, I had to rely on other fans' judgements on that, but replays later showed the ref was only a few feet away and ignored the call. When Alioski went down injured after 12 minutes, Dallas was straight up and ready to come on. As he went off so early, it felt as if we'd lost one of our sub options too early and he shouldn't have started the game in the first place. As Brentford attacked us in the initial stages, I thought they should have had a free kick at the edge of the box in front of us, but the ref said play on. He got the decision right when their player went down in the box as we clearly got the ball. The one decision, when the ball hit a Brentford player who was at least a foot inside the box, went out over the line and should have been a corner to us, was a bad decision against us. We were put on the back foot and had Casilla to thank for making a superb save to keep the scores level. The longer the game went on without us scoring, though, the worse it got, but I just wanted to keep Brentford out, especially just before half-time. Sadly for us, we let them run through us and score in the 44th minute, giving us an uphill struggle. If only Roberts had managed to equalise straight after their goal when he only had the keeper to beat it would have been a different game.

At half-time I heard Leeds fans were coming to blows with each other, sadly, due to disagreements about players. The last thing I want us to do is fight amongst ourselves. I learnt a long time ago that you will never get everyone to agree and there will always be different opinions. Even if I don't agree with them, they are still entitled to voice their opinion, as I have mine and we have to accept that without turning on each other. Agree to disagree!

The second half found us start well but then we just didn't look like scoring, although we came close in the last few minutes. The worst thing happened with Brentford scoring a second, then nearly getting a third and putting any fight back beyond us. With the home crowd taunting the Leeds fans about not going up, I was pig sick that it had come to this. Before the end I went downstairs to retrieve my flag and the Leeds fans cheered me up by singing and still getting behind the team. The club doesn't deserve the support it has in certain respects, especially for the stalwarts who have been there and seen us let down so many times before. Hearing our younger fans saying they'd travelled all this way to see this rubbish is sad.

It's not over until the fat lady sings, or so the saying goes, and I will always live in hope and support my team. I know it's hard but, although demoralised at this moment in time thinking we won't win any play-off, I will get over it in the coming days. I am proud to be a Leeds fan and as always the lack of football in the 90 minutes gets in the way of a good day out. Keep the faith no matter how hard it is. The statistics may say we have fantastic possession, but it is the end result with goals scored that counts – where we have been sadly lacking and it looks to have cost us. Next Sunday sees our last home game of the season against Aston Villa, who have picked themselves up to have a ten-game unbeaten run. As always, we need to win and you never know things could still go to the wire with Sheff Utd, despite it seeming pie in the sky at this moment. For once we had a good run with no motorway detours and I was back at home 20 minutes after midnight. I'm heading off to Guiseley to watch the under-23s tonight, where we have helped to have a sell-out crowd. It will be nice to have a break from the pressures of the Championship and see how our youngsters perform.

LEEDS UNDER-23s V NEWCASTLE
PREMIER LEAGUE CUP SEMI-FINAL, NETHERMOOR, GUISELEY, 23 APRIL 2019

Despite Leeds losing this semi-final 3-0, which I put down to me jinxing it (sorry), it was nice to go and see the game. After the pressures of the Championship, it was a refreshing change and there were lots of familiar faces there to support the team in a sell-out crowd of 3,051. It was a real family occasion for me, taking my daughter Danielle and granddaughters Hannah, Laura and Alexis with me. I managed to take a photo of the girls with Bielsa and he lifted Alexis onto the barrier so she could be seen, which was great. I said to him, 'Please stay whatever happens.' His translators who were with him were nodding in agreement. In attendance were my two sisters, Erica and Karin, nephew Mark, niece Sonya, children Tommy and Vinnie with friends, Martin,

Simon, Jessica and Tom. It was nice chatting to fans at the game and unfortunately for the pheasant, its trip to the ground ended tragically with a broken neck after hitting the stand roof before landing in front of my sisters.

Now it is back to the realities of the last couple of games where we take on Villa at Elland Road.

ASTON VILLA (H) – 28 APRIL 2019

Well it's certainly never dull being a Leeds fan, that's for sure! Today we had what I call a proper game of football, blood and thunder, with the Leeds crowd roaring the team on. Full commitment from the start from our team helped to ease the hurt felt after missing out on automatic promotion.

When I arrived at the ground with my granddaughter Hannah, we headed straight to the Peacock. I was meeting fans from all around the world today who had come to see our last game of the season. Normally I bring all my family to this game, but even when tickets came back on sale from those fans who were now not attending, I still couldn't buy any as I was a season-ticket holder and not a gold member. It was good to hear about fans who had travelled to the game from Hungary and Ireland and had initially missed out on tickets but were lucky to pick up spares yesterday. Many others who had already booked flights and accommodation were sorted in the end too, which was good. Leeds fans helping out other Leeds fans has been very noticeable recently too. I was just sending a message to the Hungarian Whites, who I was meeting, when I bumped into them in the Peacock car park. The documentary crew were there to film them, who I was supposed to be meeting later before the game. It was good to catch up with Mark and Daisy, Halifax Whites, with the latter now living in the USA. There were fans from Melbourne, Gibraltar, Argentina, Malta and Norway today, showing what a fantastic worldwide fan base we have. With us now being in the play-offs, it meant that Rita, Nikki's guide dog, had a reprieve, so today was not her last game. Rita has been going to every Leeds game for years and celebrates a goal with the rest of the fans with her barking and she will be missed when she no longer goes. Well done to Mark for wearing his costume in the name of charity, raising money for the Samaritans in memory of his friend. Also donating to Brendan Ormsby's fundraiser too meant that I supported lots of good causes today.

As I was waiting for the documentary crew to come back to the Peacock, Charley of the Harrogate Whites came to find me. Marta from Argentina, who I was looking to meet after the game, was in the tent so I caught up with her there. There were photos galore and lots of fans enjoying themselves. If I'd been sad before the game, the one thing certain to lift your spirits is being amongst other Leeds fans who love the club like I do. This is what makes following our club special and can't be beaten in my eyes. In the meantime, I found an answerphone message from West Yorkshire Police on my phone. Hannah had begged me to go into the ground as she didn't want to hang around, so I said yes. Apparently minors can't be in the ground on their own, which, although understandable, is a shame. In trying to instill confidence in our young children and giving them a bit of freedom whilst under certain conditions (I knew we were all going to sit together), it didn't work out that way. She was worried she would get me into trouble by not being with her at the time, but I will say thank you to the stewards who had to look after her as per their rules. I'll blame the documentary crew for standing me up – lol – as I would have been in the ground much earlier. As it was, I caught up with so many people that it worked out well in that regard. As well as the centenary year for Leeds United next season, it is also the centenary year for the Leeds United Supporters' Club and I love the pennant and other memorabilia they have for sale in the Peacock back room.

The team: Casilla, Ayling, Cooper, Jansson, Harrison, Klich, Bamford, Forshaw, Phillips, Dallas and Hernandez. Subs: Berardi for Dallas (45) and Roberts for Harrison (45). The final score of 1-1 Klich (72) was controversial; Leeds played to the whistle and scored, but Villa were allowed to score straight away to even the score as their player was down injured (wrong in my eyes). Attendance was 36,786, with 2,626 Villa fans.

It was lovely to see all the players bring their children on to the field as mascots when the teams came out. Ayling was buzzing with his little girl, and I could see he was up for the game from the off. Villa started brightly before Leeds got into the game, but it was one of those end-to-end games with plenty of action. The referee today lost the plot straight away and in my opinion should hang his boots up because, on what I've seen today, he should be banned from ever being a ref again. He let a couple of things go for both teams then went on a free-kick spree against Leeds by favouring Villa, with one culprit being Grealish, who spent most of his time on the floor rather than on his feet. With plenty of the free kicks being balls that Leeds won fair and square, this riled the Leeds fans up even more. The atmosphere was electric as the Leeds fans got behind their team, with both teams still looking for a goal. Casilla looked as if he'd missed a ball but then recovered to put it around the post for a corner to Villa. As Leeds were just about to break into the box in front of the South Stand, the ref blew his whistle. Just as I wondered why, everyone was going mad as he should have played advantage with our attack according to those around me, I realised that he'd blown for half-time. I can't remember the last time that I wasn't waiting for the half-time whistle to blow plus hadn't even seen the amount of injury time to play as I'd been so engrossed in the game.

If we thought the ref had been poor in the first half, he surpassed that performance in the second half. Bielsa had made two changes, with Berardi and Roberts on for Dallas and Harrison, and it nearly paid off, as we came so close to scoring when the ball went just past the wrong side of the post from Forshaw. The game had still been end-to-end, but Leeds were fighting for everything and won the ball cleanly as their player went down once again. He didn't have a head injury and the ref played on as we screamed at Leeds to keep going. That's exactly what Roberts did as he passed the ball to Klich to put the ball into the net to send the Leeds fans wild. All I could see were Villa players grabbing hold of ours and going nuts, which I couldn't understand. Why weren't they being allowed to celebrate with us? The next thing a Villa player was shown a red card, but with people standing in front of me I didn't catch what was going on at the far side of the goal, only seeing Klich being manhandled by two Villa players. From the television angles shown later, Bamford, although he had been involved in some pushing and shoving, reacted as if he'd been punched, but it didn't look like there was any contact to his face. Of the players I'd seen having a go at Klich, one of then punched him in the stomach. It was the player involved with Bamford who was red carded, although I may have missed more here, but the worst was to come on the restart. Villa were given the ball and instructed to equalise, with no one allowed to stop them, although Jansson tried. In all my years of following Leeds I have never seen anything like it, but apparently Bielsa had said to let them due to fair play. I'm sorry but this is one time I would strongly disagree with Bielsa's decision, there was no head injury and you play to the whistle. With all the cheating, diving and time wasting Villa did all through the game, it should have been just desserts. To say Bielsa had been booked earlier – for what I've no idea – he is more magnanimous that I would ever be, but there was no need to be as we hadn't done anything wrong again! The ref showed how inept he was as he should have stuck with his decision of awarding a goal. As long as it doesn't affect us playing the away leg of the play-offs on the Saturday it will be fine in the long run, but if points matter? I won't go there as I'd be very angry. We nearly got the 'winner' in the last few moments as the game ended in a draw.

We stayed to see the players walk around the pitch at the end of the game and the talking point with everyone we met afterwards was letting Villa walk the ball in the net. Unbelievable! That said,

I really enjoyed the game today, plus it passed by ever so fast with everything going on. Football is not a non-contact sport and you should be able to challenge for a ball without a free kick being given, because the opposition fall down at the drop of a hat. Football should not be for namby pambys who cheat their way through a game, give me a proper football game any day. I have been asked to mention Terence Bell and Debbie Hood, who helped Jay Patel and his wife from London get tickets for the game today. I wished a safe trip home to our Bournemouth Whites, Steve and Bev, plus the same goes for all the other fans I'd met near Billy's statue. I also caught up with some more Leeds fans back in Halifax when I met my family at The Wainhouse Tavern for tea. It just shows that wherever we go, there will always be some Leeds fans!

With Norwich and Sheffield United gaining automatic promotion, we face the play-offs once more. I have to take some of my own advice here; I'd once said when we played man u at Old Trafford in the FA Cup that if we go there expecting to lose we always will do. Go out and play to win and lo and behold Beckford scored to make that dream happen. The same goes for the play-offs with our poor record. We should not be scared of anyone, we have shown today that we can still play well and will for once be the underdogs. It's time for us to change that record and make it happen, so come on Leeds, you can do it! Our last league game sees us travel to Ipswich and I'm still looking forward to a good day out.

CHAPTER 11

IPSWICH (A) – 5 MAY 2019

After hearing Bamford had got a two-game suspension for simulation after the Villa game by the FA, it came as no surprise that Hourihane from Villa had got away with the punch on Klich. Because he stayed on his feet, it was deemed not to be a punch, surprise, surprise. Leeds put in a defence for Bamford, asking for the ban to be lenient due to us letting Villa score. That should never have formed our defence as I still maintain that goal should not have been handed to them on a plate. Instead we should have asked for Villa to be brought up for bringing the game into disrepute by attacking our players and punching Klich for scoring a perfectly legitimate goal and playing to the referee's whistle. As video evidence appeared on social media showing the punch on Klich, there was no excuse for not charging them. Also on view was Villa scoring a goal with a Stoke player down recently, where Villa happily took the goal. When the boot was on the other foot they didn't make a fuss at all and showed how two faced they are.

As for today's game, it may have had no meaning, but it always had the typical Leeds United banana skin waiting as Ipswich were already relegated and we needed one point to confirm our final place as third in the Championship. As usual we lost against ten men, missed a penalty and let Ipswich score three goals. After a 4.30am get up, well, what's another kick in the teeth? Thousands

of Leeds fans still turned up to celebrate our season and had been in good spirits, with plenty coming down for the weekend, but many coming for the day only. As it turned out, we ended up third as both Villa and West Brom lost, with Derby taking the last play-off spot to be our opposition in the semi-finals, with the away leg first. My publisher is a Derby fan and as I want Leeds to go through and win these ties, plus the final at Wembley, please let him be the disappointed one. Whatever happens, we have to do this even if it is the hard way.

The stewards were very friendly letting me go downstairs to the front of the stand to put my flag up, with one proclaiming he was a Leeds fan too. I caught up with the documentary crew too and had a chat with them before realising I was being filmed again, oops!

The team: Casilla, Ayling, Cooper, Jansson, Klich, Forshaw, Roofe, Phillips, Harrison, Dallas and Hernandez. Subs: Clarke for Harrison (61). Leeds lost 3-2, with Klich (45) and Dallas (76) scoring for Leeds. Attendance was 20,895, with 3,963 Leeds fans.

Leeds took the game to Ipswich and played some good football, the only downfall being our final weak passes that allowed them to clear the ball, and when we did have a shot we didn't get any on target. As the game went on we started being too casual at the back and Ipswich came close to scoring before Forshaw had a shot saved by their keeper. I could see that we were giving Ipswich hope and that was going to be dangerous for us. The next thing I saw, Casilla raced out of his area to the wing as Ipswich attacked but there was no way he was going to get anywhere near both their player and ours. As he brought their player down, my heart sank as I thought this was another sending off for him, but luckily for Casilla he only received a yellow card. Why he keeps doing the same thing, I have no idea, but he really needs to think about what he is doing as this was costly for us once again. With Ipswich scoring from the resulting free kick, what could be worse? I'm sure I'd seen a stat about them not scoring or winning for a long time and these stats usually change when they come up against us. We did still try and came close when Roofe had a shot blocked, before a further attack just before half-time saw Klich hit a strike from the edge of the box into the net. That was a relief to know we'd scored just before the break.

Sadly, we didn't keep the impetus up because within a couple of minutes of the second half starting Ipswich scored a second goal. That was just what we didn't need! When Clarke came on as sub we upped our game and started attacking more, coming close with the ball flying all over the box, but without us putting it into the net. An Ayling cross once again brought a second goal for Leeds after Roofe had hit the bar before Dallas got on to the end of it to equalise. Someone said we'd settle for a draw and I said no we would go out to win. When we were awarded a penalty and their player was sent off, Roofe got hold of the ball to take it. My only thoughts were to make sure we scored from it. Well it certainly didn't go to plan as Roofe slipped as he went to take it and the ball flew over the top – another penalty miss and another one that wasn't even on target to force a save from their keeper. To say we were never awarded penalties in the early part of the season, now we have missed four out of our last six. Once again this proved to be very costly for us as Ipswich

scored three goals in a single game for the first time this season, scoring three goals from three shots on target (courtesy of @LUFCDATA). With another mix up in our defence between Ayling and Casilla, Ipswich were able to get the winner just before full time.

As play-off tickets go on sale tomorrow, I'm just glad that I have got the auto cup scheme for both home and away tickets. Although I would be guaranteed a ticket for both legs, I don't have the hassle of worrying about it. Good luck to the Leeds United youngsters in their game at Elland Road tomorrow. I won't be attending this time as I jinxed them at Guiseley recently, making them lose, and I want them to win. Who knows what the play-offs will bring against Derby, but we must do it the hard way once again. Surely it will go right for us this time … please …? One thing is for sure, we'll know soon enough.

The good thing about today was being with others, supporting each other and catching up on sleep. With friends going through similar issues to me at the moment with family members, I wish them all the luck in the world. Personally, we made some progress with my husband this week, taking one step forward then two steps back. Keep fighting everyone and that includes Leeds United!

DERBY COUNTY (A), PLAY-OFF SEMI-FINAL, FIRST LEG – 11 MAY 2019

On Wednesday I was having my nails done and it was really funny when I was introduced to the lady next to me, as she was a Leeds fan too. The two of us were chatting away about Leeds United with Hannah and Debbie looking at us both saying that they hadn't a clue what we were on about lol. Thank you Paula, who it turned out had worked at Elland Road for 17 years, for buying my book *Back to Reality, Leeds United 2017-18*. After another hard week for my family, this culminated with the death of my father-in-law yesterday. The good thing was we all managed to get there and spend some time together and I was there holding his hand when he took his last breath. There are many others going through traumas of their own today, not only friends but those families who suffered in the Bradford Fire disaster and the death of young Leeds fan Ian Hambridge at Birmingham in 1985. My heart goes out to all of them on what was a dark day for football all those years ago. It was also my friend Karen's birthday which sends a poignant reminder every year.

As I pulled my car onto the street I couldn't believe my eyes seeing that little ba****d magpie walking across the road in front of me. At first I thought damn, then I decided that I needed to kick that superstition into touch today. After a tearful conversation with my youngest daughter, then another with my eldest daughter, I was glad to get that out of my system. Whilst standing at the bar when we stopped in Chesterfield on our way to the game, someone asked me how we would do and I just shrugged my shoulders. At that time it felt like it was an effort to go to the game and getting into the play-offs is something I could have done without. As my daughter Dani and I struggled to get a table in the packed pub, we were lucky to join Nikki, Stephen and Rita the dog

at their table. By the time we left after food, drink and plenty of conversations in good company, my spirits had lifted and I was looking forward to getting there.

We arrived in plenty of time for kick-off and I headed to the front to put my flag up. There were lots more put up before the game and they are great to see. As I stood there, Katherine Hannah from BBC Radio Leeds came to see me for an interview plus asked for another one at the end of the game. My mum and sister Karin heard the first one and my sister Erica the second one. I also did an interview for the Leeds United documentary crew. Although slightly nervous at this time, I said I wanted to win 4-0 today, 4-0 on Wednesday and 4-0 at Wembley. That is just because I want the other team to be out of sight and out of mind to ease the nerves. I just wanted Leeds to give 110 per cent like my hero Billy Bremner always used to, and my new mantra is saying 'it's not over till it's over, so we still have a chance'. Seriously I just wanted to win the game and as I won the football card on the coach I said it was a good omen!

The team: Casilla, Ayling, Berardi, Cooper, Dallas, Forshaw, Roofe, Klich, Phillips, Hernandez and Harrison. Subs: Shackleton for Forshaw (went off injured 24) and Clarke for Roofe (81). Leeds won the game 1-0 with a goal from Roofe (55). Attendance was 31,723, with 2,780 Leeds fans. With Jansson out injured Berardi stepped in to take his place. It was good to see all our injured players had travelled to the game to support the team too.

We played towards the goal nearest the Leeds fans in the first half, and to me it was noticeable that Derby were looking to gain an advantage by keeping the team at the far end of the pitch when

warming up too. I just thought we'd have to shut them up instead! I thought we played well in the first half, and although we had lots of possession again we weren't able to put the ball into the net. What was good though was seeing Leeds do exactly what I wanted by fighting for every ball, and although Derby got the chance to attack a few times they didn't come close to scoring as we battled to keep them out. I hadn't put my glasses on so, although I could see the players at the far end of the ground, I did miss things. The most important thing was not seeing Forshaw go off injured and Shackleton coming on as a substitute. I thought he'd been playing from the start and I'd missed it, oops! Derby were also battling to keep Leeds out and the first half was a good one to see as we went in at half-time on equal terms.

The second half saw us attacking the far end and Derby started falling like flies looking for and getting the free kicks. When Derby fouled our player as we attacked, the ref said play on. With that, Harrison put a great cross over to Roofe in the middle of the goal mouth to hit the ball into the net and send the Leeds fans into raptures. There were bodies flying all over the place as I dodged them to stay upright. There were fantastic scenes of joy amongst the Leeds fans and it was great to be part of it. Roofe was unlucky not to score a second goal minutes later, but their keeper made the save to prevent him getting another one. I started getting a little nervous as the game went on and couldn't believe it when their player went down in the area and a penalty was given. I was convinced we hadn't fouled their player as the ref went over to speak to the linesman at the far side of the pitch. I said 'Wouldn't it be great if he changed his mind and said it wasn't a penalty?' With that the decision was reversed as the Leeds fans cheered and the Derby fans jeered. It was great to see the replays on social media afterwards confirming that Harrison was fouled and hadn't touched their player anyway. After Derby's short spell, which had me on tenterhooks, Leeds got the better of them again as the whole team battled and got to the end of injury time with a 1-0 win. What better tonic did I need than that? I also loved the chant today, 'All of the spies, are hidden away, just try not to worry, you'll beat us some day, we beat you at home, we beat you away, stop crying Frank Lampard, stop crying Frank Lampard!' That was class and whoever made it up full credit to you as I can't stop singing it. Thank you also to those fans who love what I do with my blog and as always your comments are appreciated and that is also a big boost for my self-esteem.

Getting a goal was great as it gives us a psychological advantage. Let's make Elland Road a cauldron of hate in the second leg and scare the living daylights out of Derby.

DERBY COUNTY (H), PLAY-OFF SEMI-FINAL, SECOND LEG – 15 MAY 2019

With one thing after another happening kicking you when you are down, together with grid-locked roads all around us, it was a relief to get to Elland Road in time for kick-off. The one thing it did, though, was give me no chance to worry about the game ahead of us. I knew once the game

kicked off that I would be able to forget about things for a while, but I felt we'd missed out on the build-up to the atmosphere. With only a one-goal lead, there was still hope at this point that we'd do this and, although slightly nervous, the tie was in our hands. I'd be happy when it was 10pm, though, then at least we'd know for certain what happened next. The stat I'd found incredulous on Saturday was that of the 46 games we had been in the automatic promotion spots in 42 of them.

It didn't take long to start taking photos and it was nice to be thanked for sharing my blog by one fan who had been caught on camera a few times this season. Getting into the Kop, there was a great atmosphere below the stand that started to get the juices flowing. Leeds fans all over the ground had been given a scarf on our seats today, which was a nice gesture by Leeds, and Victor Orta had been putting them out personally. They reminded me of the silk scarves we used to wear in the 70s, so thank you for that. As the teams came out to a crescendo of noise, it felt like something we had never witnessed before. Despite having attended games for over 50 years, this will take some beating and would be up there with the best. Scarves twirling or held up, it was a fantastic sight and something I will always be proud of being part of.

The team: Casilla, Cooper, Ayling, Berardi, Phillips, Hernandez, Harrison, Bamford, Shackleton, Dallas and Klich. Subs: Clarke for Klich (86) and Brown for Bamford (88). Leeds lost the game 4-2, with Dallas getting a brace for us (24 and 62). Attendance was 36,326, with 2,653 Derby fans. Leeds lost on aggregate 4-3, meaning Derby meet Villa in the Championship play-off final at Wembley.

With the Leeds crowd in full voice, it took a while for us to settle into the game and I certainly didn't want Derby to get an early goal. It was vital we gave them nothing, then Dallas put the ball into the net in front of the South Stand after Cooper's header had hit the post, giving us a two-goal cushion on aggregate. We were unlucky not to get a second goal when Klich's shot hit the cross bar but bounced down on the wrong side of the goal-line. I didn't realise that Bamford was booked for diving as I'd decided not to bother wearing my glasses, superstitions and all that! Whilst we'd kept attacking (the best form of defence) I'd not been worried about Derby at all. The last five minutes or so saw us slack off for some reason. We then hit the self-destruct button once again when Casilla made an error coming out as Cooper was trying to shield the ball and let Derby in to score right on half-time. That was the difference between going in with a two-goal lead, but instead we had given Derby a lifeline. Casilla did exactly the same thing a short while afterwards, nearly presenting Derby with another goal. Why he has to continuously hare out of his goal when he has no chance of getting near the ball is beyond me. The teams went off at half-time with expletives ringing in Casilla's ears from me!

The second half had barely kicked-off when Derby scored again to equalise on aggregate – all because of that goal before half-time in my eyes, which was a crucial one not to give away. We should have taken the lead again when Harrison had a great chance, only to see the ball kicked off the line before Dallas brought a save out of their keeper. There were shouts from everyone around me that we should have had a penalty for hand ball. Although I didn't see it myself, fans around me

said it was blatant but no officials made the decision. A penalty was awarded to Derby a short while later, when their player went down in the area, and they sent Casilla the wrong way to put them 3-1 up on the night. What a turnaround for Derby, but so predictable from Leeds, sadly. The game wasn't over though, as Dallas got his second goal of the night to equalise on aggregate. With the tie looking to go into extra time and penalties, neither of which I wanted, we were reduced to ten men when Berardi was sent off. We'd been fouled twice and the ref played on before Berardi got his revenge and a red card. As we regrouped, Derby started to attack us and Bamford was robbed of the ball by being too lightweight. They then put the final nail in the coffin by scoring their fourth on the night, putting an end to our promotion hopes. Once again, with the game in our hands, we threw away that opportunity. I only had slight stomach churning, probably because I'd seen it so many times before. We were so close yet so far away. I found that I wasn't as upset as I thought I'd be, probably because I was resigned to the failure once again. As I pointed out to Hannah, my granddaughter, this is part of being a Leeds United fan and how it prepares you for being a good loser. Character building it is called. It was a bit of a tongue-in-cheek saying it this time, though, because I was adamant we had to gain promotion this year; our best chance for years and we'd thrown it away. My ambition for this season had always been aspire for the top two and go up automatically as we had to get promoted this year otherwise we would never do it.

Only time will tell how we pick ourselves up for next season in the Championship. For me there will be no excuses, but it has to be automatic promotion and champions. Matching this

257

season's performances will be hard with all the injuries we have suffered to the squad. Replicating most of the games will depend on who is part of our squad going forward. A must is we have to keep Phillips and not cash in on him. We have to build the team around him and our other youngsters and have some older heads amongst them. I'm not happy with Casilla tonight and, as I said all those months ago, I would have kept Peacock-Farrell in goal as we had to build our team around the youngsters and I would have made Casilla fight for his place. Whether he has got too complacent I don't know, but seeing his suicidal charges out of goal have made me scream at him for his incompetence.

As someone who won't be going on the Australian pre-season tour, I hope everyone has a great time. I would love to have been part of it but cannot be. We must have a flying start to next season and recruitment will be a vital part of that. I will be taking a break for a few weeks from my blog but will turn it into a book and season review in due course for those who are interested. I will post details up when available.

To all those fans who have supported me, had photos taken, chatted, or just been part of following Leeds United, I thank you all and appreciate all you have done to help me through some tough times. Although these are not over yet, and won't be for a long time, I salute you all. Just keep the memory of the sight of our fans in the stands at the start of this game and realise that it is special being a Leeds fan. Our support is unique and don't ever lose that feeling. See you all next season – LUFC – Marching on Together.

CHAPTER 12

FIXTURES AND RESULTS
SEASON 2018-19 – 57 GAMES AND FINAL COMMENTS

The good news is that Marcelo Bielsa has agreed to stay at Leeds United for the forthcoming season. That to me is the continuity I have craved for a long time because I feel it is the only way we will move forward. My ambition last year was to aim for automatic promotion, which we came so close to doing. This year I want exactly the same but for us to gain promotion in our centenary year. Have high aspirations and you have a better chance of achieving your aim.

After having pre-season games at both York and Guiseley it was good to get back to the football and meeting up with friends again. The ones I was unable to make were the pre-season tours to Australia and Italy. As much as I would love have to been in Australia, it made me feel really sad that I wasn't there when I saw all the Leeds fans posting on social media. There were some fantastic photos and postings with many familiar faces, and I was definitely jealous! Sadly, I cannot do everything that I want to and will have to be envious of my friends who did go to them.

I was also sad to see Pontus Jansson sold and I thank him for re-connecting the team with the fans as that was something that had been missing for a long while beforehand. Seeing it now with the way the players have interacted with our fans on the same flights or on trips around Perth and Sydney has been excellent. They have made a lot of our fans very happy.

I am looking forward to us carrying on with the way we started last season. Although there were many ups and downs, as usual, as long as the players wear their shirts with pride and play for them and us, there is hope. Being able to play for 90 minutes has been better as the players are fitter and the only downside was the many long-term injuries impacting on the season for us.

Fullerton Park Supporters' Club will once again be my travelling companions to away games with people I have known for a long time. I will be looking out for fans who want to have their photos taken for my blog on my travels and also at Elland Road. I want to thank all the fans who contribute to my blog, whether they are in the photos or reading it from afar. All their comments and input are greatly appreciated. See you there! LUFC – Marching on Together!

FIXTURES FOR THE SEASON 2018-19 – 57 GAMES

DATE	OPPOSITION	VENUE	COMPETITION	SCORE	ATT	SCORERS
17.7.18	Forest Green Rovers	New Lawn	Pre-season friendly	1-2	3,250 1,161 Leeds fans	Roofe 16 Ayling 25
19.7.18	York City	Bootham Crescent	Pre-season friendly	1-1	4,400 approx. 2,000 Leeds fans	Sam Dalby 58
22.7.18	Southend United	Roots Hall	Pre-season friendly	1-1	3,815 988 Leeds fans	Ayling 34
24.7.18	Oxford	Kassam Stadium	Pre-season friendly	4-3	4,772 1,335 Leeds fans	Roberts 54 Baker 63 Clarke 71
26.7.18	Guiseley	Nethermoor Park	Pre-season friendly	3-4	3,366 approx. 1,800 Leeds fans	Klich 39 Clarke 49 Edmondson 53, 71
29.7.18	Las Palmas	Elland Road	Pre-season friendly	1-0	11,499 approximately 30-50 Las Palmas fans	Roofe 86 Vieira's last game transferred to Sampdoria two days later
5.8.18	Stoke City	Elland Road	Championship	3-1	34,126, 2,471 Stoke fans	Klich 15 Hernandez 45+1 Cooper 57
11.8.18	Derby	Pride Park	Championship	1-4	27,311 2,000 Leeds fans	Klich 5 Roofe 21, 60 Alioski 64
14.8.18	Bolton	Elland Road	*Carabao Cup first round*	2-1	19,617 1,007 Bolton fans	Bamford 27 Saiz 35
18.8.18	Rotherham	Elland Road	Championship	2-0	33,699 707 Rotherham fans	Luke Ayling scoring his first league goal 49 Roofe 72
21.8.18	Swansea	Liberty Stadium	Championship	2-2	20,860 approx. 2,100 Leeds fans	Roofe 40 Hernandez 79
25.8.18	Norwich	Carrow Road	Championship	0-3	25,944 approx. 2,500 Leeds fans	Klich 21 Alioski 26 Hernandez 67
28.8.18	Preston	Elland Road	*Carabao Cup second round*	0-2	18,652 approx. 1,000 Preston fans	First defeat of the season under Bielsa's management
31.8.18	Middlesbrough	Elland Road	Championship	0-0	35,417 2,322 Boro fans	Leeds remain top of the league going into the International break

DATE	OPPOSITION	VENUE	COMPETITION	SCORE	ATT	SCORERS
15.9.18	Millwall	New Den	Championship	1-1	17,195 2,220 Leeds fans	Harrison 89
18.9.18	Preston	Elland Road	Championship	3-0	27,729 306 Preston fans	Cooper 37 Roberts 74, 82
22.9.18	Birmingham	Elland Road	Championship	1-2	34,800 1,314 Birmingham fans	Alioski 85
28.9.18	Sheffield Wednesday	Hillsborough	Championship	1-1	26,717 4,600 Leeds fans	Klich 62
2.10.18	Hull City	KCOM Stadium	Championship	0-1	13,798 2,100 Leeds fans	Roberts 51
6.10.18	Brentford	Elland Road	Championship	1-1	31,880 510 Brentford fans	Jansson 88
20.10.18	Blackburn	Ewood Park	Championship	2-1	20,029 7,717 Leeds fans	Klich 45+1
24.10.18	Ipswich	Elland Road	Championship	2-0	29,082 approx. 500 Ipswich fans	Roofe 22 Cooper 66
27.10.18	Nottingham Forest	Elland Road	Championship	1-1	34,308 1,766 Forest fans	Roofe 84
4.11.18	Wigan	DW Stadium	Championship	1-2	14,799 4,856 Leeds fans	Hernandez 9 Roofe 46
10.11.18	West Bromwich Albion	The Hawthorns	Championship	4-1	25,661 2,737 Leeds fans	Hernandez 90+2
24.11.18	Bristol City	Elland Road	Championship	2-0	34,333 889 Bristol City fans	Roofe 69 Hernandez 86
27.11.18	Reading	Elland Road	Championship	1-0	27,806 197 Reading fans	Dallas 60
1.12.18	Sheffield United	Bramall Lane	Championship	0-1	25,794 2,243 Leeds fan	Hernandez 82
8.12.18	QPR	Elland Road	Championship	2-1	33,781 approx. 300 QPR fans	Roofe 45+3, 53 (first penalty since September 2017)
15.12.18	Bolton	The Macron Stadium / University of Bolton Stadium	Championship	0-1	17,484 4,550 Leeds fans	Bamford 66
23.12.18	Aston Villa	Villa Park	Championship	2-3	41,411 approx. 2,500 Leeds fans	Clarke 56 Jansson 61 Roofe 90+5
26.12.18	Blackburn Rovers	Elland Road	Championship	3-2	34,863 1,378 Blackburn fans	Williams own goal 33 Roofe 90+1, 90+4
29.12.18	Hull City	Elland Road	Championship	0-2	35,754 2,145 Hull fans	

DATE	OPPOSITION	VENUE	COMPETITION	SCORE	ATT	SCORERS
1.1.19	Nottingham Forest	The City Ground	Championship	4-2	29,530 approx. 2,000 Leeds fans	Clarke 52 Alioski 64
6.1.19	QPR	Loftus Road	*Emirates FA Cup third round*	2-1	11,637 3,148 Leeds	Halme 25
11.1.19	Derby County	Elland Road	Championship	2-0	34,668 1,238 Derby fans	Roofe 20 Harrison 47
19.1.19	Stoke City	The Bet365 Stadium	Championship	2-1	28,586 2,919 Leeds fans	Alioski 90+5
26.1.19	Rotherham	The New York Stadium	Championship	1-2	11,259 2,317 Leeds fans	Klich 51, 86
2.2.19	Norwich City	Elland Road	Championship	1-3	36,524 2465 Norwich fans	Bamford 90+1
9.2.19	Middlesbrough	The Riverside Stadium	Championship	1-1	30,881 approx. 4,500 Leeds fans	Phillips scoring for Leeds 90+11
13.2.19	Swansea	Elland Road	Championship	2-1	34,044 approx. 400 Swansea fans	Jansson 20 Harrison 34
23.2.19	Bolton Wanderers	Elland Road	Championship	2-1	34,144 approx. 500 Bolton fans	Bamford 16 (pen) Alioski 68
26.2.19	QPR	Loftus Road	Championship	1-0	14,763 3,105 Leeds fans	
1.3.19	West Bromwich Albion	Elland Road	Championship	4-0	35,808 approx. 2,500 WBA fans	Hernandez 20 seconds, Bamford 28 & 63 Alioski 90 + 2
9.3.19	Bristol City	Ashton Gate	Championship	0-1	24,832 2,680 Leeds fans at the game 2,000 at the beam back at Elland Road	Bamford 9
12.3.19	Reading	The Madejski Stadium	Championship	0-3	17,701 2,071 Leeds fans	Klich 14 Hernandez 22, 43
16.3.19	Sheffield United	Elland Road	Championship	0-1	37,004 2,641 Sheffield United fans	
30.3.19	Millwall	Elland Road	Championship	3-2	34,910 975 Millwall fans	Hernandez 34, 83 Ayling 71
6.4.19	Birmingham City	St Andrews	Championship	1-0	24,197 2,781 Leeds fans	
9.4.19	Preston	Deepdale	Championship	0-2	18,109 with 5,516 Leeds fans plus those in their end / corporate areas	Bamford 62, 76

DATE	OPPOSITION	VENUE	COMPETITION	SCORE	ATT	SCORERS
13.4.19	Sheffield Wednesday	Elland Road	Championship	1-0	36,461 2,527 Sheffield Wednesday fans	Harrison 65
19.4.19	Wigan	Elland Road	Championship	1-2	34,758 743 Wigan fans	Bamford 17
22.4.19	Brentford	Griffin Park	Championship	2-0	11,580 1,680 Leeds fans	
28.4.19	Aston Villa	Elland Road	Championship	1-1	36,786 2,626 Villa fans	Klich 72
5.5.19	Ipswich	Portman Road	Championship	3-2	20,895 3,963 Leeds fans	Klich 45 Dallas 76
11.5.19	Derby County	Pride Park	*Championship play-off semi-final first leg*	0-1	31,723 with 2,780 Leeds fans	Roofe 55
15.5.19	Derby County	Elland Road	*Championship play-off semi-final second leg*	2-4 Leeds lost 4-3 on aggregate. Derby meet Villa in the Championship play-off final at Wembley	36,326 2,653 Derby fans	Dallas 24, 62

CHAMPIONSHIP TABLE 2018-19

		P	W	D	L	F	A	GD	PTS
1	Norwich City	46	27	13	6	93	57	36	94
2	Sheffield United	46	26	11	9	78	41	37	89
3	**LEEDS UNITED**	**46**	**25**	**8**	**13**	**73**	**50**	**23**	**83**
4	West Bromwich Albion	46	23	11	12	87	62	25	80
5	Aston Villa	46	20	16	10	82	61	21	76
6	Derby County	46	20	14	12	69	54	15	74
7	Middlesbrough	46	20	13	13	49	41	8	73
8	Bristol City	46	19	13	14	59	53	6	70
9	Nottingham Forest	46	17	15	14	61	54	7	66
10	Swansea City	46	18	11	17	65	62	3	65
11	Brentford	46	17	13	16	73	59	14	64
12	Sheffield Wednesday	46	16	16	14	60	62	-2	64
13	Hull City	46	17	11	18	66	68	-2	62
14	Preston	46	16	13	17	67	67	0	61
15	Blackburn Rovers	46	16	12	18	64	69	-5	60
16	Stoke City	46	11	22	13	45	52	-7	55
17	Birmingham City	46	14	19	13	64	58	6	52
18	Wigan	46	13	13	20	51	64	-13	52
19	Queens Park Rangers	46	14	9	23	53	71	-18	51
20	Reading FC	46	10	17	19	49	66	-17	47
21	Millwall	46	10	14	22	48	64	-16	44
22	Rotherham United	46	8	16	22	52	83	-31	40
23	Bolton Wanderers	46	8	8	30	29	78	-49	32
24	Ipswich Town	46	5	16	25	36	77	-41	31

BV - #0007 - 271219 - C0 - 234/156/14 - PB - 9781780916019